Primary Sources in the Library

A Collaboration Guide for Library Media Specialists

Mary J. Johnson

Linworth
PUBLISHING, INC

Dedicated to My Mother
Arleyne Lundy Gildersleeve

Library of Congress Cataloging-in-Publication Data

Johnson, Mary J., 1949-
  Primary sources in the library : a collaboration guide for library
media specialists / by Mary J. Johnson.
       p. cm.
Includes bibliographical references and index.
  ISBN 1-58683-075-9
  1. School libraries--Activity programs--United States. 2. Media
programs (Education)--United States. 3. History--Study and teaching
(Elementary)--Activity programs--United States. 4. History--Study and
teaching (Secondary)--Activity programs--United States. 5. Archival
materials--United States. 6. History--Sources. 7. United
States--History--Sources. I. Title.
  Z675.S3J645 2003
  027.8'222'0973--dc21
                            2003012887

Published by Linworth Publishing, Inc.
480 East Wilson Bridge Road, Suite L
Worthington, Ohio 43085

ISBN: 1-58683-075-9

5 4 3 2

Table of Contents

Table of Figures

Acknowledgments

I wish to thank my generous Academy School District Twenty colleagues for supporting this project through your kind words, valuable feedback, and willingness to test primary source lessons with real students. To Linda Thompson, my American Memory partner, what a delightful journey we have shared! To the capable librarians in my school com munity, you are steadfast champions for kids and learning. Because of you, administrators at every level support our vision. I am lucky to work with the best of them, especially my principal, Ross MacAskill. To my amazing library and technology staff, you are truly unequalled! To Donna Miller, my Linworth editor, your steady guidance has made my first publishing experience both pleasurable and rewarding. Finally, to Roger Hayden Johnson, my husband, my unending love and gratitude for your constant support and encouragement.

Introduction

In the summer of 2000, Mary Johnson spent a week at the Library of Congress as an American Memory Fellow learning how to integrate primary source materials into the curriculum, and her library life changed forever. The skills she had honed in three decades of teaching and librarianship suddenly converged in engaging, inquiry-based, primary source lessons that struck a chord with students of the digital generation.

Primary Sources in the Library: A Collaboration Guide for Library Media Specialists encourages both beginners and experienced librarians to add primary source expertise and resources to their library programs. As an "in-the-trenches" librarian herself, the author has experienced the daily challenges that confront librarians when they try to implement new teaching strategies and form productive partnerships with classroom teachers. Using the practical lessons and suggestions in this book to introduce primary source concepts to students and colleagues, library media specialists can begin experimenting with their own primary source collaborations. One step at a time, they build their own repertoire of primary source projects, customizing each lesson in the book to match the teachers and students in their own school environments.

Primary Sources in the Library: A Collaboration Guide for Library Media Specialists takes library media specialists through the current maze of educational trends to establish their central position as leaders of inquiry-based learning through primary source lessons. Throughout the book, readers will find applicable content standards, strong assessment tools, organizational strategies, and hints for working successfully with teaching partners. Relying on the strengths of librarians as curriculum generalists, the lessons bridge multiple content areas and work across many grade levels, from 4th through 12th grades and beyond. More than a simple list of Web sites and lesson plan links, this book focuses on building the expertise of each reader in searching, bookmarking, and applying digital skills to develop primary source collections and curriculum. In a speech before the Colorado Educational Media Association, Doug Johnson, author of *The Indispensable Librarian: Surviving (and Thriving) in School Media Centers in the Information Age*, reinforced the importance of the library media specialist's online primary source skill set: "Librarians are the interface to digital primary resources. This role adds value to our positions. Flaunt it!" (Johnson "Indispensable").

Librarians stand poised to lead their schools in designing innovative digital approaches to teaching and learning. Thus the first chapter explains why librarians should seize the opportunity to become the online primary source specialists for their schools. The library media specialist's role in promoting the use of primary sources in the classroom often depends upon specialized skills in locating and repackaging those sources for harried and overextended teachers. Of course, no library media specialist can succeed without first building collaborative relationships with teachers. The second part of the first chapter covers specifically how to apply a collaborative model to primary source lesson planning.

Activities in the second chapter introduce primary source concepts to different age levels, while the third chapter offers a more extensive family artifact activity that helps students solidify and personalize their understanding of primary sources in real life.

Even though schools have used computers in teaching and learning since the mid-1980s, only more recently have teachers and library media specialists begun to understand the structures that promote inquiry-based learning with digital information. Specialized techniques for analyzing and applying primary sources, as well as significant curriculum and standards issues, will be considered in the fourth chapter.

For those library media specialists who can't wait to begin collaborating with teachers on their own exciting new primary source curriculum, the remaining chapters offer a wide variety of lessons and ideas that can be applied to nearly every grade level (with modifications, of course) and every curricular area. Primary sources hold enormous promise for the teaching of history and so much more. Readers will look at a school-wide "Patriotic Speech Festival," historical letter writing units, a multimedia presentation on the history of technology, an American landscape painting and geography lesson, and other unique, cross-disciplinary combinations.

Each lesson is complete, flexible, and highly practical. An index helps readers locate the perfect theme or content area for the teacher who just happens to walk in the door in need of a creative teaching idea. Each chapter ends with a useful checklist of proactive ideas for "The Primary Source Librarian in Action."

The final chapter, "Bringing It Home — The Local Primary Source Librarian," looks at current local and regional trends in primary source librarianship. Readers will study the field of museum education and build a resource bank of museums, historical societies, and cultural facilities in their own communities. They will also examine issues of partnering with community institutions to deliver primary source instruction.

Primary Sources in the Library: A Collaboration Guide for Library Media Specialists gives library media specialists the tools to become the primary source experts in their schools. Through the power of primary source collaborations, library media specialists will energize their curriculum, their students, and their schools.

Chapter

1

The Librarian Connection

Primary Sources Play to a New Audience

Library media specialists first noticed the reviews in *The Book Report* and *School Library Journal*. Publishers promised to make history come alive through the latest online or print collections of primary documents. Students could now "directly touch the lives of people in the past" ("History in the Raw," par. 1). Newly-ordered library books arrived increasingly filled with photographs and diary entries and political cartoons, pulling stories from "the dust-bin of history" and endowing them "with character, personality, and texture" (Greenwood 4). Primary sources were pushing their way to center stage as stars of the latest educational publishing house productions.

Online subscription database services that had made the leap to full text not so long ago suddenly touted fantastic new primary source collections available at the click of a mouse:

> … provides access to more than 41,000 fascinating primary source docu-
> ments, letters, diaries, government documents, speeches, photographs,
> maps, audio clips and video clips…provides historical context and a per-
> sonal connection to noteworthy events and experiences (Student Resource
> Center—Gold).

Even that staple of the school library reference collection—the encyclopedia—offered extensive primary source collections in its latest CD-ROM or online version. Additionally, within the last half dozen years, excited rumors began to circulate about a Web site called American Memory that made the vast primary source collections of the Library of Congress available to students and teachers regardless of geographic location. Articles in professional journals claimed that students could access more than one million items through American Memory in their new roles as student historians.

In a few short years, primary sources had moved from the rarified realm of doctoral studies in history to become a significant new force in K–12 curriculum and instruction. Hands-on, Web-based primary source sessions began to appear on professional library conference agendas, and school librarians carried the medium, the message, and the definition of primary versus secondary sources back to their schools:

Primary Source: Firsthand evidence of historical events or periods.

Secondary Source: A later interpretation of historical events or periods.

Heeding the accumulating voices urging educators to teach with primary sources, library media specialists ordered the books. They subscribed to the online services. They installed the latest CD-ROM encyclopedias. They even went online to explore the American Memory site, losing themselves in hundreds of photographs and old film reels and hundred-year-old diaries. Unfortunately, in spite of their personal delight in discovering primary sources, school librarians undoubtedly sensed a chasm between their own curiosity-driven enjoyment and the actual student use of the new resources.

A Powerful Set of Skills

Librarians have always collected resources. Teachers have always used those resources to support classroom learning. Traditional educators might question why the library media specialist should now suddenly assume responsibility for the use of primary sources across the curriculum, outside the library, and beyond the long-established role of the library media specialist as a mere provider of resources. The visionary library media specialist who has for decades fought outmoded perceptions of libraries as book warehouses will enthusiastically seize the opportunity to become the school's primary source specialist and a primary source partner with equally innovative teachers. Whether they know it or not, library media specialists already possess a powerful set of primary source skills:

1. As a technologist, the library media specialist already functions as the school expert in online search strategies and analysis of online sources as well as a leader in technology training and modeling the use of information technologies for student learning. In an astonishingly short time, primary sources have swept onto the digital stage, requiring the mix of technology skills that librarians have already perfected through thousands of hours of dedicated online study and practice.

2. As an information specialist, the library media specialist continually matches resources—print, digital, audio, and now primary—with the information needs of students and teachers. "As information specialist, the library media specialist provides leadership and expertise in acquiring and evaluating information resources in all formats; in bringing an awareness of information issues into collaborative relationships with teachers, administrators, students, and others; and in modeling for students and others strategies for locating, accessing, and evaluating information within

and beyond the library media center" (*Information Power* 5). Primary sources simply add a rich layer to the information specialist's collection of resources.

3. As an unbiased observer of the total school curriculum and culture, the library media specialist assumes the role of a non-threatening partner with teachers interested in co-developing curriculum using primary sources. This curriculum collaboration owes its success to the library media specialist's instructional leadership and experience but also to the library media specialist's skills in human relations. The last part of this chapter will focus on the social behaviors and understandings that contribute positively to collaborative relationships.

4. As a school and community leader, the library media specialist influences public perceptions of school quality, innovation, and achievement. The potent combination of libraries and technology in support of primary source lessons carries weight with a technologically savvy school community. Primary source lessons also offer multiple opportunities for the library media specialist to celebrate innovative curriculum publicly and to raise the prestige and visibility of teacher partners. Many of the projects outlined in this book offer suggestions for community outreach and communication.

Fostering Inquiry-Based Libraries and Classrooms

Students can only discover the joys of primary sources within a learning environment that encourages and celebrates inquiry, an environment in which teachers design instruction to help students engage in active learning. The reality is that few schools today share a school-wide culture of inquiry. "As presently constituted ... many schools, from kindergarten through graduate school, reflect a preference for keeping students passively in their seats, listening to presentations of information they need to memorize and return in toto when asked. But there is hope for creating cultures of inquisitiveness within our schools" (Barell 42). Because librarians witness active learning from real-world resources on a daily basis, they can play a pivotal role in leading their schools to create "cultures of inquisitiveness."

When asked to recall their most memorable teacher and classroom experiences from kindergarten through high school, one group of high school seniors consistently praised the teachers who had designed lessons that were experiential, inquiry-based, active, curiosity-driven ... by whatever name, the memorable lessons shared the same characteristics (Bertel, personal interview). Primary sources can play a part in the reform from teacher-centered, textbook-driven curriculum to the kind of discovery-based learning that students remember.

The Bay Area National Digital Library Fellows Project, in conjunction with the Bancroft Library at the University of California Berkeley, brought together teacher and librarian teams from twelve San Francisco area schools to design and test student lessons with digitized primary resources. Director Kathleen Ferenz reported the results of this four-year program of research and development in a message to the Library of Congress American Memory Fellows listserv:

> Using multiple sources from digital libraries for instruction is best used in
> inquiry oriented classrooms. Inquiry oriented classrooms need new structures
> and forms of collaboration among students and the teacher. We call this

building community. Building community in the classroom expressly focused on inquiry will change the look and feel of the learning environment by: (3)

- changing how students and teachers interact with each other.
- making questions as important as answers.
- requiring a diverse repertoire of instructional techniques and assessments by the teacher.
- making the classroom environment a welcome place for everyone to learn and exchange ideas.
- promoting respect, responsibility, and clear reasoning.
- engaging more students in higher order thinking skills.
- allowing for more students to engage in challenging tasks and distribute the learning so that the knowledge is not held by one person, but created collaboratively by many.
- allowing students to make meaningful connections between the content and their lives.

Ferenz goes on to state that the "use of primary historical resources (whether real or digital) in classrooms fosters inquiry and innovative teaching strategies because these raw materials provoke so many questions" (3).

When students drive the inquiry, teachers must become comfortable with ambiguity. When kids are in charge of their learning, the outcomes become more difficult to predict because the roles of teacher as authority and student as passive recipient of the teacher's knowledge are reversed. Sara Lawrence Lightfoot, a noted Harvard professor of education, points out, "In our schools, students are mostly trained to get to the answer quickly. Part of teaching is helping students learn how to tolerate ambiguity, consider possibilities, and ask questions that are unanswerable" (157). Unanticipated questions require more resources— yet another opportunity for the library media specialist to step in as a provider of materials and a guide to their use.

The textbook, long the purveyor of total course content, has gradually moved to a lesser role, making way for more "uncoverage" than "coverage," a concept promoted by Grant Wiggins and Jay McTighe, experts in assessment as well as curriculum and instruction. They view the role of the school textbook as changing from a simple syllabus to a valuable but hardly unique resource and reference. In their opinion, "The textbook is seen as one resource, supplemented as needed with primary-source materials" (131).

Over twenty years ago, in a lengthy report on the American high school, the Carnegie Foundation for the Advancement of Teaching decried excessive reliance on textbooks and instead recommended expanded use of original sources: "Most textbooks present students with a highly simplified view of reality and practically no insight into the methods by which the information has been gathered and the facts distilled. Moreover, textbooks seldom communicate to students the richness and excitement of original works. When students are privileged to read the primary sources, they meet authors personally and discover events first hand" (Boyer 143). The wheels of school bureaucracies spin slowly, but now some two decades after the Carnegie report was issued, teachers and library media specialists can more easily match increased access to primary sources with their new understandings of how children learn best through inquiry.

Primary sources do indeed promote inquiry-based learning. In a 1999 comparison study of two different elementary schools that received an infusion of materials and training to improve school library programs through the DeWitt-Wallace Readers' Digest Fund's "Library Power" program, the school that fostered inquiry significantly outperformed its counterpart (Oberg 1). The following description of inquiry learning from the case study could well serve as a credo for primary source learning:

> From a constructivist viewpoint, inquiry learning should involve exploration and developing personal connections with what is being learned. From both the constructivist and the information search process perspectives, inquiry-based learning should begin with the children having background knowledge of the topic or developing that background in ways that develop children's interest in and commitment to the topic. Once children have developed their knowledge of and interest in the broad topic, they should be involved in determining what questions will be investigated and how they might find the information they need about a particular topic selected from the broad topic area. Children should be involved in making sense of information, presenting what they have learned in their own words or drawings and/or in other information formats chosen because of their appropriateness to purpose. (Oberg 8).

Exploration, personal connections, background knowledge, questions to investigate, finding information, making sense of information, presenting new knowledge in the student's own terms—all of the elements of inquiry-based learning exist within primary source lessons. Even more exciting, the library media specialist has the means to transform learning within a school from dry, prescribed content to far more innovative instructional practices. Unfortunately, some library media specialists inadvertently inhibit rather than promote the transformational power of inquiry-based learning. The next section places the responsibility for the transformation squarely on the librarian's shoulders, with a little help from essential friends.

The Library Media Specialist's Responsibility

"The old school library as the resource room down the hall where students go once a week for library lessons or to check out a book is a model of the past. In the information-age school, the library is an extension of the classroom, integrated into the curriculum, providing opportunities and resources for students to pursue their lines of inquiry and construct their own meanings" (Kuhlthau 9). As more and more resources become digitized, students and teachers enjoy new information options unbound by time or by a library facility. To remain viable as information intermediaries, library media specialists must recognize the shift toward greater reliance on electronic sources of information and develop thoughtful strategies for managing them proactively.

Online collections of digitized primary sources are expanding daily, and they require the same professional skills of selection and evaluation as any print collection. Some library media specialists mistakenly view electronic resources as a threat, when in fact they extend and enrich library collections. Current collection development practices should support increased access to primary source materials, both print and electronic.

With a quality primary source collection in place, the strong library media specialist remains constantly on the lookout for opportunities to integrate primary sources into teaching and learning. Keenly aware of educational trends, the professional librarian recognizes that nearly every recent educational reform can benefit from the inclusion of primary sources. For example, primary sources fit superbly with theories of inquiry-based learning, constructivism, discovery learning, and information literacy. Lessons that integrate primary sources also meet dozens of content standards, as the second chapter will demonstrate. Primary source lessons promote differentiated instruction, and library media specialists and teachers can select the sources carefully to meet all learning styles and intellectual levels in support of the "No Child Left Behind" philosophy of today's politicians. Indeed, the library media specialist who facilitates the use of primary sources supports all educational reforms that value authentic inquiry over traditional lecture delivery, regardless of the current educational jargon that labels the movement.

Finally, primary sources equal authentic learning. In discussing how teachers can use primary sources to facilitate learning, Girod and Cavanaugh state that teachers "must shift their thinking from boldfaced words and questions at the end of the chapter to situated activities and subject matter ideas, real-world tasks, and authentic performance tests. Primary sources offer a sense of the real world that can be used in pedagogically powerful ways" (42).

Overcoming Barriers to Collaboration

In order to function as a catalyst in the transformation to inquiry learning through primary sources within a school, the library media specialist must absolutely understand collaboration and its relationship to change within organizations. In other words, people working *together* change organizations. People working *separately*, no matter how hard, smother change, or at the very least, limit that change to isolated incidences.

Much like an administrator, the library media specialist sits in a crow's nest, able to observe and learn from a broad range of teaching and learning styles as well as personalities. In almost all cases, the success or failure of beginning primary source lessons has everything to do with the library media specialist's relationships with teachers and almost nothing to do with primary source expertise. That relationship can range anywhere from the childhood lament—"You're not the boss of me!"—to a healthy and productive professional relationship that thrives on collaboration. Even in schools with a history of successful collaborations between the library media program and teachers, any honest library media specialist will admit to failures and disappointments in trying to work with some colleagues.

Successful library media specialist/teacher collaborations occur over time and build upon shared experiences. Rarely do they begin at the instigation of the teacher. Even though "collaborations" imply shared responsibility, somebody must initiate them, and thus, the library media specialist must remain constantly alert to opportunities whenever and wherever they may occur. Collaborations do not always mean an enormous commitment to a long-term project, and library media specialists should not reject minimal or even one-shot opportunities to experiment with primary source collaborations. "Quick and dirty" *is* worth the trouble as long as it introduces primary sources as an option for learning.

Primary sources imply new experiences for both teachers and library media specialists, actually making early primary source interactions less risky than stepping on a teacher's established content area expertise. Generally when teachers and library media specialists first work together to test a primary source lesson, neither party wields an unhealthy "power" over the other. In fact, the library media specialist can propose a joint project that gives both parties a chance to be recognized as innovative curriculum leaders. Fully aware of the need to acknowledge the teacher's own particular expertise, the library media specialist defers to the teacher as an instructional partner still in charge of classroom management, differentiated instruction for individual students, and content expertise. Even when 90% of the credit goes to the classroom teacher, the co-conspirator approach allows the library media specialist to break into the kingdom of the classroom, clearing the path to future collaborations using primary sources. It is an investment.

From a pedagogical standpoint, one additional hurdle remains. Most teachers teach as they have been taught, and few have personally interacted with primary sources during the course of their own educational experiences. Teachers who have neither experienced nor observed teaching with primary sources will naturally resist materials and methods outside their comfort zone. Their discomfort might manifest itself in concerns about increased teaching load, a perceived or real lack of access to computers, resistance to the unpredictable results of inquiry, loss of classroom control, and pressures to finish the textbook or cover all mandated standards. To attain any level of collaboration, it is vital that the library media specialist acknowledge these concerns. The library media specialist must then work diligently to turn the potential intimidation of primary source teaching into a journey of joint risk taking and professional growth—share the risk, share the rewards.

As an ally in support of student learning, the library media specialist not only encourages innovative teaching with primary sources but also frees classroom teachers from the isolation and lack of recognition that is so often their lot. "Teaching is a very autonomous experience—but the flip side of autonomy is that teachers experience loneliness and isolation. Teachers tend to miss other adult company, colleagueship, relationship, criticism, camaraderie, support, and intellectual stimulation. There must be time and space in school days for teachers to come together to support one another, to respond critically to one another, and to develop plans together" (Lightfoot 165). A neutral, uncritical, and supportive library media specialist can quite effectively pull teachers out of their isolation while co-creating exciting new primary source lessons.

Figure 1.1 (page 8) shows a "Primary Source Collaborative Lesson Plan" form that the library media specialist might use to guide the first contact with a classroom teacher who expresses an interest in incorporating primary sources into lessons. Following the procedures listed below, the library media specialist uses the form as a reminder and guide throughout the collaboration:

- The library media specialist fills in the basic plan during the actual collaboration conversation, then makes a quick copy to hand to the teacher-partner.
- If the library media specialist has convenient access to a computer, the form can be saved as a template and filled out electronically before printing it immediately for both parties.

Figure 1.1: Primary Source Collaborative Lesson Plan

Primary Source Collaborative Lesson Plan

Dates:	Teacher:
Times:	Content Area:
# Classes Per Day:	Assignment Name:

Overview of Primary Source Lesson

Student Tasks

Final Product/Assessment

Primary Sources/Other Resources/Training Required

Notes

Classroom Teacher	Technology Staff	Library Staff

- As the teacher or library media specialist adds details, the library media specialist provides up-to-date copies with changes.
- When the library media specialist gains a clear understanding of the student tasks and final assessment, a list of content standards along with technology and information literacy standards can be added to the planning form.
- Teachers receive the official-looking lesson plan with expectations and activities clearly outlined plus a complete list of standards for their files and their administrators.

Without the support of administrators, the library media specialist will inevitably meet additional resistance to the notion of primary source collaborations, which usually suggest risky and untested methods. The principal who highlights successful primary source lessons in faculty and parent meetings sends a message that this is one small curricular reform worth considering. The library media specialist must work to keep the principal informed through formal and informal conferences, regular reports or newsletters, copies of notes congratulating teachers who collaborate on primary source lessons, and even public performances or exhibitions of student primary source projects. When the library media specialist, the teacher, and the principal build shared meaning out of primary source lessons, they all start to own the collaboration.

Understanding Collaboration As a Part of School Change

Much has been written about school change, and the library media specialist who makes a point of studying change within organizations will be far better prepared to manage the frustrations as well as the opportunities of collaboration. In any collaboration, it is absolutely essential to meet teachers where they are and to build upon their sense of competence. One researcher on change in schools, Dr. Robert Evans, writes, "Alterations in practices, procedures, and routines hamper people's ability to perform their jobs confidently and successfully, making them feel inadequate and insecure, especially if they have exercised their skills in a particular way for a long time (and even more if they have seen their performance as exemplary)" (32). The teacher who views himself as having applied textbook and lecture methods artfully and effectively may interpret the external imposition of primary source lessons as questioning his competence.

Close observation of the instructional planning process helps the library media specialist identify where it happens, when it happens, and how it happens. Primary source collaborations, like any other joint projects, must fit into the natural rhythm of the planning process. Furthermore, practicality is essential even when the library media specialist appears willing to take on major tasks, from collecting and preparing copies of primary sources to identifying standards. As Evans points out, "Implementation happens during the school year and after the school day—there is no closing the factory to retrain the workers" (85). In other words, most innovation and curricular change in the school organization occurs on the fly. Successful library media specialists recognize this reality and work with it rather than against it. They also recognize that "When it comes to innovation, participation is a primary path to commitment: people are much more likely to invest themselves in something they help shape" (Evans 231). If collaboration forces the teacher to create a new role that reflects someone else's idea of effectiveness, why shouldn't the teacher be resistive? Nothing inhibits collaborations more than an arrogant library media specialist. Teachers must own the change.

The Primary Source Librarian in Action

To begin building the foundation for primary source learning, library media specialists buy and subscribe to print, electronic, and online resources that feature collections of primary sources. They apply their well-honed skills in the use of educational technologies, online searching, information retrieval, collection development, curriculum leadership, teacher/library media specialist collaboration, and marketing and public relations. The primary source librarian consciously follows the steps below to transform the school environment into one rich with primary source learning.

The Primary Source Librarian's Checklist:

- ❑ Purchase print materials and subscribe to online services that feature primary sources.
- ❑ Self-train or attend formal training in using online collections such as American Memory.
- ❑ Build upon established skills as a technologist, information specialist, curriculum collaborator, and school and community leader to establish credibility as a primary source librarian. Market those skills.
- ❑ Research the larger context of school reform and the inquiry-based learning that lies at the heart of most student-centered reforms, and discover the best fit for primary sources.
- ❑ Work with teachers and administrators to build a shared culture of inquiry in which primary sources lead to personal questioning of history and events.
- ❑ Research primary source lesson plans, collecting ideas for multiple curricular areas.
- ❑ Keep a keen eye on primary source integration opportunities. Listen. Propose. Beg. Give strategic support. Do the work. Whatever it takes!
- ❑ Consciously build collaborative skills through patience, enthusiasm, and a willingness to defer to teachers, who are, after all, the content experts.
- ❑ Begin collaborations with the shared goal of improving student learning, but recognize that primary source partnerships imply redefined roles, a threat to long-held beliefs about teaching methods, and the risk of unpredictable answers.
- ❑ Use the lesson form presented in **Figure 1.1** to help clarify the collaborative process.
- ❑ Keep the principal informed of primary source efforts and successes, and invite the principal to observe lessons.
- ❑ Celebrate every primary source success publicly. Share with parents, administrators, departments, students, technology leaders, and all other willing listeners and readers.
- ❑ Always credit the teacher who took the primary source risk.

Even when library media specialists follow all the preliminary steps to becoming primary source librarians, without superb collaborative skills, they will fail to transform learning into an inquiry process that engages students. Forced to endure static textbook presentations, students will miss the quality learning engendered by creative primary source collaborations between teachers and library media specialists. The responsibility for changing the status quo falls to the library media specialist. The primary source librarian, working in partnership with capable colleagues, can transform a school, kid by kid, primary source by primary source.

Chapter

2

Introducing Primary Sources

Primary and Secondary Sources Defined

The definition of "primary sources" varies from narrow to broad depending upon one's perspective as a historical purist or as a practitioner driven by practical classroom considerations. Most often, long lists of examples follow even the shortest definitions. Lists help students identify examples from their own lives, thus personalizing primary sources and prompting students to expand the lists based on their own family evidence.

First, the definition. The Yale University Library defines a primary source as "firsthand testimony or direct evidence concerning a topic under investigation" (par. 4). Primary sources are created contemporaneously to an event or phenomenon, without the benefit of hindsight and further experience from which to judge them. In short, eyewitnesses produce primary sources.

In contrast, secondary sources add an interpretative level to the primary sources on which they are based. They are "generally at least one step removed from the event" (Whitson, par. 10). In "Using Primary Source Documents in the Classroom," the Ohio Historical Society further explains that they were created by "someone either not present when the event took place or removed by time from the event" (par. 7). Developers of secondary sources gather evidence, organize, analyze, and repackage the information for a particular audience. Textbook writers produce secondary sources. So do students.

The first chapter offered simple definitions of primary and secondary sources (see page 2) that teachers and librarians can use as a point of departure for discussion, particularly when students try to sort sources that often fall into gray areas. The examples in **Figure 2.1** clarify and extend the definitions.

Figure 2.1: Primary Source Examples

Maps	Pamphlets	Posters	Advertisements

Newspaper Articles	Personal Letters	Diaries	Prescriptions

Wills	School Records	Guest Registers	Memberships

Financial Records	Census Records	Oral Histories	Speeches

A Sampling of Primary Sources

Historians depend heavily upon *written* documents as primary source evidence. Fortunately, a broader definition that includes visual as well as written media permits educators and students to develop a particularly flexible and useful list for the classroom because it encompasses everyday artifacts. Students are limited only by their curiosity and creativity as they imagine all the firsthand evidence around them.

The broad definition also opens the door to developing primary source curriculum, particularly for elementary and middle-level students. For example, a beginning reader can "read" an advertisement for a revolutionary new marble shooter, but not the first draft of the U.S. Constitution. A high school student strong in visual literacy skills following years of extensive television, film, and other visual media experiences is quite capable of interpreting an early film of immigrants disembarking at Ellis Island. He can then extend the visual introduction by reading an immigrant oral history. To ignore the expanded definition would be to miss an important opportunity to connect to the personal lives of today's students.

The "Primary Source Examples" in **Figure 2.1** will help students envision the potential range of choices, although it is by no means an exhaustive list.

The National Archives and Records Administration (NARA), one of the richest repositories of American primary source documents, lists many categories beyond the more obvious letters, diaries, maps, and official reports pictured in **Figure 2.1**. For example, NARA's "The Digital Classroom" Web site identifies the items in **Figure 2.2** below as qualified primary sources.

Figure 2.2: NARA Primary Sources

Broadsides*	Editorial/political cartoons	Foreign language documents
Government proclamations and resolutions	Graphs and charts	Interviews
Leaflets	Patents	Petitions
Popular ballads	Press releases	Forms
Resolutions	Surveys	Telegrams

Broadsides—sizable sheets of paper printed with political messages, advertisements, or popular ballads on one or both sides.

It takes only moments to personalize the list. As trivial as their own daily residue may seem to them, students quickly make connections to their own lives. Whether or not any of this primary life evidence qualifies as valid historical data for future historians remains open to judgment. Nevertheless, the collected production does represent a life—a life that generates a history. The library media specialist and teacher can use the rather traditional list offered in **Figure 2.1** and expanded by the National Archives in **Figure 2.2** to jumpstart student thinking as they examine their daily routines and activities. Through a simple brainstorming exercise, students will quickly add personal items to the list, as seen in **Figure 2.3**.

Figure 2.3: Personal Primary Sources

Baby books	Birth announcements	Birthday cards
Bus passes	Concert tickets	Doodles in notebooks
E-mail messages	Films	Graffiti
Homework assignments	Invitations	Lunch tickets
Notes passed in class	Old cookbooks	Paintings
Phone messages	Photographs	Postage stamps
Postcards	School programs	Songs
Souvenirs	Trading cards	Wrapping paper

Primary Sources and the Standards-Based Curriculum

In the current educational environment of standards and accountability, both teachers and library media specialists sense a new pressure to teach history through primary sources. For example, the National Center for History in Schools clearly requires in Standard 4 that students conduct historical research in the following ways:

A. Formulate historical questions from encounters with historical documents, eyewitness accounts, letters, diaries, artifacts, photos, historical sites, art, architecture, and other records from the past.

B. Obtain historical data from a variety of sources, including: library and museum collections, historic sites, historical photos, journals, diaries, eyewitness accounts, newspapers, and the like; documentary films, oral testimony from living witnesses, censuses, tax records, city directories, statistical compilations, and economic indicators.

C. Interrogate historical data by uncovering the social, political, and economic context in which it was created; testing the data source for its credibility, authority, authenticity, internal consistency, and completeness; and detecting and evaluating bias, distortion, and propaganda by omission, suppression, or invention of facts.

D. Identify the gaps in the available records and marshal contextual knowledge and perspectives of the time and place in order to elaborate imaginatively upon the evidence, fill in the gaps deductively, and construct a sound historical interpretation. (*National Standards for History, Basic Edition, 1996*)

Educational standards in other content areas, such as the *Standards for the English Language Arts* developed by the National Council of Teachers of English and the International Reading Association, also require that students "gather, evaluate, and synthesize data from a variety of sources (e.g., print and non-print texts, artifacts, people) to communicate their discoveries in ways that suit their purpose and audience" (Standard 7). Later chapters will show that primary source materials support a wide range of content area standards that reach far beyond the obvious history curriculum.

Chapter

3

My Family Artifact

A Personal Look at Primary Sources

Everyone leaves memories behind in the form of "artifacts," such as journals, family possessions, photographs, papers, and other personal items. Traditionally, educators have limited
most primary source lessons to written documents, particularly at the advanced placement
high school level with its required "document-based questions," or DBQs. Futurist David
M. Levy takes a broader view when discussing the term *document*: "*Writing* and *written
form* tend to suggest alphabetic materials and therefore leave out (or downplay) photographs,
drawings, paintings, maps, and other nonverbal forms of expression" (6). At the early stages
of teaching the concept of primary sources, it is more effective to create lessons around
"nonverbal" artifacts than written documents.

Looking at family artifacts gives students a way to see themselves, to understand
their heritage through the surrounding context. What part did a special family artifact play
in the family's own story? What does it say about a particular ancestor or about the family's
place in history? The effectiveness of this chapter's "My Family Artifact" lessons lies in
hands-on activities that connect the student to everyday, personal experience. Like Velcro,
the exercises help students hook their family research to previous knowledge and personal
interest, then extend to higher-level historical research. "Cognitive researchers often refer to
these tasks as 'authentic' activities to distinguish them from the kinds of fragmented, artificial exercises often found in schools" (Viadero 34). There is nothing fragmented or artificial
about Grandma's wedding dress or Great Uncle Herbert's pipe. Furthermore, by the end of
the "My Family Artifact" activities, students will have cemented their understanding of the
concept of primary sources.

Figure 3.1: Our Memories, Our Artifacts

Our Memories, Our Artifacts

- All of us leave memories behind.
- Look around your house, your attic, your cellar.
- What memories do you see?

Family Photographs?

Journals or Diaries with Recollections of...

- Babies?
- Weddings?
- Work?
- Local news?
- World events?
- Holidays?

Manuscript Diary of Margaret A. Eadie, 1901-1909
http://www.library.upenn.edu/etext/collections/diaries/eadie/

Family Papers?

- Family Bibles
- Diplomas
- Invitations
- Newspaper Clippings
- Letters

Family Possessions?

- Clothing or Needlework
- Toys
- Furniture
- Tools
- Works of Art
- Glass
- Ceramics

What do these artifacts tell us about our own family stories?

Who?   Where?

What?   Why?

When?   How?

Setting the Stage with Good Questions

Educational researchers and practitioners have studied and written extensively about the importance of beginning lessons with good questions. "In our schools, students are mostly trained to get to the answer quickly. Part of teaching is helping students learn how to tolerate ambiguity, consider possibilities, and ask questions that are unanswerable" (Lightfoot 157). When researcher David Ruenzel observed classroom discussions in public schools, he noted, "The teacher would ask a question, but it was clear he already knew what the answer would be; it was an open-and-shut question" (21).

In this chapter's "My Family Artifact" lessons, the students discover their own answers. They also learn that the quality of their questions about the artifact and its place in the family directly impacts the depth of their answers. Through a modeled practice activity, the library media specialist and teacher lead students, unused to thinking about questioning techniques, to improve upon even the most basic and familiar "*who, what, when, where, why,* and *how*" questions. But first, students may need to revisit the concept of artifacts.

Re-Introducing Artifacts

To remind students that primary sources can include a wide range of artifacts, the library media specialist and teacher can either lead a discussion (see Chapter Two: "Introducing Primary Sources") or design a simple visual presentation similar to the "Our Memories, Our Artifacts" PowerPoint presentation seen in **Figure 3.1**.

Using the discussion questions in **Figure 3.2**, the library media specialist and teacher invite students to brainstorm what artifacts surround them in their daily lives.

Figure 3.2: Exploring Our Artifacts

---

1. If you look around your homes, do you see any "memories" in the form of artifacts?

2. Do you have any furniture that has been passed down through your family?

3. Do you have any old clothing, toys, works of art, dishes, newspaper clippings, diaries, or letters that might bring with them a family story?

4. Have you or anyone in your family ever collected rocks, bottles, feathers, ceramic dogs, model furniture, stamps, tiny shoes, thimbles, baseball cards, Star Wars figurines, or any other items that are still in your home?

5. What family treasures would you want to show your friends if they visited your home?

Figure 3.3: Artifact Question Worksheet

Artifact Question Worksheet

Student Name _____

Title of Artifact:	Collection Name:
Write questions below:	**Write answers below:**
Who	
What	
When	
Where	
Why	
How	
Extended Research Question:	**Ideas for Research:**

©Academy School District 20, Colorado Springs, CO. Used with permission.

Next, the library media specialist uses a computer projection system to take students on a visual tour of the American Memory collections (http://memory.loc.gov), demonstrating that artifacts may include photographs, posters, sheet music, playbills, advertisements, works of art, letters, and much more. In addition to showing some of the astonishing breadth and depth of the American Memory collections, this activity allows the library media specialist to model some basic search techniques unique to this remarkable Web site. (The professional library media specialist will never regret having dedicated time and effort to become an expert at searching the American Memory site. It is a skill with long-term impact on student and teacher success, not to mention the important perception of the library media specialist as an online primary source expert.)

Next, the library media specialist asks the entire group of students to choose one online artifact for a practice analysis. With the item projected on a screen, the library media specialist models simple who-what-when-where-why-how questioning techniques as students fill out the "Artifact Question Worksheet" in **Figure 3.3**.

Modeling Questions, Modeling Quality

Students typically have trouble writing specific historical questions, so modeling becomes essential. For example, students might write, "When is it?" rather than "When was the photograph taken?" or "What is he wearing?" rather than "What is the man in front of the fence on the left side of the photograph wearing?" This is a good time to remind students that their answers also need to be specific because as student historians, they are writing for an audience beyond their immediate family. "This quilt was given to my great grandmother for her wedding" does not include the necessary historical detail. Instead, students need to document all relevant information in as much detail as possible: "This quilt was given to my great grandmother, Mary Elizabeth Allen, as a wedding gift when she married Thomas G. Lundy on September 10, 1917."

The grid in the **Figure 3.3** "Artifact Question Worksheet" includes a final "Extended Research Question" box that invites a higher level of analysis than the traditional "just-the-facts, please" list of who, what, when, where, why, and how questions. A curiosity-driven question, it pushes students to examine in more depth the historical context of an artifact, and the question's quality helps determine the extent of further research required. For example, a student who analyzes a collection of depression glass for the final project can research the simple questions of when it was made and why, who sold it, and what gives it its special look. The "Extended Research Question" might also ask about the economic conditions that made the glass so popular during the Great Depression. In another example, a student whose great grandfather took photographs with a Brownie Kodak camera (the artifact) can expand his research by asking about the history of the Eastman Kodak company and its impact on photography. The "Extended Research Question," if stated well, encourages the student to look beyond the simple facts provided by the immediate family.

Before moving on to the next phase of "My Family Artifact," the teacher and library media specialist should check for understanding by reading some of the extended research questions and helping students to improve upon wording and content. Are the questions silly or truly researchable? Do they seek to extend knowledge? Can students preliminarily identify sources of answers? In an ideal world with adequate Internet access, students would

Artifact Practice Activity

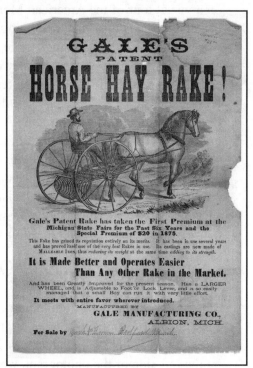

Goal: To examine and analyze an "artifact" from one of the *American Memory* collections of the Library of Congress.

Instructions:

1. Select an "artifact" from one of the American Memory online collections. This artifact may be a photograph, poster, song, movie, interview, playbill, newspaper article, advertisement, work of art, letter, map, or any other item that might have been donated to the Library of Congress by one of your ancestors.

   http://memory.loc.gov

2. Print a copy of the artifact and attach it to the Artifact Question Worksheet.

3. Write (A) the title of the artifact and (B) its collection name in the boxes provided at the top of the Artifact Question Worksheet.

4. Research the artifact by reading about the condition, by reading any bibliographic information that accompanies the artifact, or by using other online or print resources.

5. Write complete "who, what, when, where, why, and how" *questions* about the artifact, followed by an Extended Research Question.

6. Write a complete *answer* to each "who, what, when, where, why, and how" question. (For the practice worksheet, do not research the Extended Research Question, but be prepared to suggest potential sources that would help you answer it.)

Due Date: _____

follow the American Memory search demonstration and the modeled practice questions with searches of their own in a computer lab or even on wireless laptop computers. The "Artifact Practice Activity" in **Figure 3.4** introduces students to just such a follow-up individual or paired practice activity in which students search for and select an American Memory artifact to analyze.

In this activity, students print a copy of the artifact and attach it to a blank copy of the **Figure 3.3** "Artifact Question Worksheet" grid. Next they write a new set of questions, including an extended research question. As they begin their search for answers, they find clues to help interpret their chosen artifact by reading about the larger collection, by mining any bibliographic information that accompanies the artifact, or by referring to other online or print resources.

Before moving on to the final "My Family Artifact" project, the library media specialist and teacher conduct an interim assessment, pointing out questioning techniques that need improvement as well as incomplete answers or sloppy work. The simple "Artifact Activity Checklist" assessment in **Figure 3.5** on page 28 helps the teaching team identify students who have not yet grasped the concepts of asking significant questions and supporting answers with evidence before they begin the final project with a real artifact.

"My Family Artifact" Final Project

After the brainstorming activities and the practice analyses, students will be impatient to discover artifacts in their own families. Like elementary school show-and-tell time, the "My Family Artifact" final project gives students an opportunity to share meaningful pieces of their lives, scarcely aware that they are in reality doing basic historical research.

The idea of researching actual items from the past is hardly a new one. In a 1926 textbook entitled *Modern Methods in High School Teaching*, professor Harl R. Douglass wrote, "The relic is to the history class what the specimen is to the science class. Old newspapers and documents, weapons, garments, and pieces of furniture are quite interest-provoking, and in many instances result in a better grasp of the subject-matter. Students may find these in their homes and those of their neighbors, and often a useful collection may be gathered together for a period-display in the schoolroom" (232).

In the plan for the "Family Artifact Final Project" in **Figure 3.6** on page 29, students take responsibility for their own artifact for just one day—the day they bring the artifact to school for a digital camera photo shoot or a lesson in scanning. The added digital or scanned photograph requirement not only helps students avoid fear of losing precious family heirlooms in public displays, it also adds technology experience to their personal skills. Students continue to build technology skills as they manipulate the digitized images in their final word-processed artifact displays.

When the students begin to research their own family artifact, the library media specialist and teacher distribute a follow-up worksheet with slight changes that reflect the personal nature of the artifact. In the "Family Artifact Questions" handout in **Figure 3.7** on page 30, for example, a box that asks for the artifact's relationship to the family has replaced the "Collection Name" box from the previous American Memory practice worksheet. The bottom right box asks students to list potential resources for learning about their artifact.

Figure 3.5: Artifact Activity Checklist

Artifact Activity Checklist

Each checklist item=5 points

List of Tasks	✓	Points
1. "Artifact" selected and printed from American Memory online collections and attached to worksheet.		
2. Title of artifact written in box provided on worksheet.		
3. Full collection name written in box provided on worksheet.		
4. Who? Complete question and answer.		
5. What? Complete question and answer.		
6. When? Complete question and answer.		
7. Where? Complete question and answer.		
8. Why? Complete question and answer.		
9. How? Complete question and answer.		
10. Extended Research Question completed (but not answered).		
	Total Points =	/50

Figure 3.6: Family Artifact Final Project

Family Artifact Final Project

Introduction:

All of us leave memories behind in the form of "artifacts"—journals, photographs, papers, family possessions, and so on. If you look around your homes, you will probably see such "memories." Do you have any furniture that has been passed down through your family? Do you have any old clothing, toys, works of art, dishes, newspaper clippings, diaries, or letters that might bring with them a family story?

You have already completed a practice worksheet on an artifact from the *American Memory* pages of the Library of Congress Web site. Now you are ready to begin your own family artifact analysis.

Goals:

1. To examine and analyze an "artifact" from your own family.
2. To scan or take a digital photograph of the family artifact.
3. To produce a word-processed document which includes the digitized family artifact and a complete analysis of the family artifact (who, what, when, where, why, and how questions and answers plus one extended research question and answer). Projects will follow good design principles.

Instructions:

1. Choose an "artifact" from your own family.
2. Bring the artifact to school to take a digital photograph of it (or scan it if it is a two-dimensional item such as a photograph, drawing, or letter). If you have your own digital camera, you may bring a photograph of your artifact on disk.
3. Fill in the "Artifact Question Worksheet" with the name of your artifact and a short description of the item and its relationship to your family.
4. Fill in the worksheet with "who, what, when, where, why, and how" **questions** that apply to your artifact.
5. Fill in the worksheet with your researched **answers** to your "who, what, when, where, why, and how" questions.
6. Write and research an "Extended Research Question" about your artifact and its place in history.
7. After your teacher approves your preliminary worksheet, complete # 8 below.
8. Create a one-page word-processed document that includes the digitized artifact, all questions, and all answers in an attractively designed format.

Figure 3.7: Family Artifact Questions

Family Artifact Questions	Student Name _____
Name and Description of Artifact:	**Artifact's Relationship to Family:**
Write questions below:	**Write answers below:**
Who	
What	
When	
Where	
Why	
How	
Extended Research Question:	**Ideas for Research:**

The teacher and the library media specialist might choose to complete their own family artifact analysis as a model for students to follow. Referring to the photograph of the diphtheria quarantine sign in the final project instructions (**Figure 3.6**), for instance, the author completed the model "Family Artifact Example" in **Figure 3.8** on page 32 to show to students, who studied and critiqued the example before filling out their own worksheet.

Students find a remarkably varied and fascinating selection of family artifacts to analyze. The following list of actual examples highlights the variety of items discovered by just one class:

- A toy fire truck given as a gift in 1949.
- A grandfather's lariat.
- A photograph of a horse and buggy school bus with the student's great-grand-mother standing in front.
- A scrapbook of photographs taken by a great grandparent who was a Red Cross worker in Albania during World War I.
- Purple rhinestone-encrusted "cat-eye" spectacles from the 1950s.
- A girl's diary detailing personal reactions to the assassinations of John F. Kennedy and Martin Luther King, Jr.
- A baby's barrette with tiny teeth marks in it.
- A newspaper article about an 84-year-old Irish immigrant who returned to Ireland and gained some local fame when he dug his own grave.
- A grandfather's flight jacket and cap covered with World War II medals.
- A great grandmother's hand-embroidered wedding handkerchief.

Each one of the above artifacts precipitated family discussions that excited students and helped them connect, some for the first time, to stories of ancestors and discoveries of family tales never before passed on to the current generation. In some cases, one simple arti-fact led to the sharing of still more family secrets, enriching the student's understanding of the family's place in history and connecting the student to grandparents and parents in whole new meaningful and intellectual ways.

In the culminating assignment, students transfer the content of their worksheet grids to word-processed documents. Although not essential to the analysis goals of the project, the word processing activity adds an important technology component, including manipulation of the digitized artifact image. Whether word-processed or handwritten and pasted together, the final presentation requires students to make critical decisions about order, what to include or exclude, how to present the research through solid historical writing, and how to add visual interest. The "Final Rubric—My Family Artifact" in **Figure 3.9** on pages 34 and 35 covers questioning, research, technology, writing, and design goals.

The Primary Source Librarian in Action

In an article on "Literacy and Learning for the Information Age," Carol Kuhlthau writes, "Students must be engaged in problems and projects that involve them in raising questions, seeking information from a wide variety of resources, changing their questions as they learn more, identifying what they need to know more about, demonstrating what they have

Family Artifact Example

Name and Description of Artifact:	Artifact's Relationship to Family:
Photograph of Quarantine Sign	*Nailed to tree at my great-grandparents' farm in Iowa in 1926.*
Write questions below:	**Write answers below:**
Who *had a disease that made the quarantine sign necessary and who diagnosed the disease?*	*My grandmother, Arleyne Lundy Gildersleeve, 6 years old, diagnosed with diptheria by "Old Doc Mills," McCallsburg.*
What *were the symptoms and what was the treatment?*	*Began with sore throat. Doc Mills recognized "membrane" after no cases in many years; treated with an "antitoxin."*
When *was the quarantine sign put up and when was it removed?*	*Family was quarantined for 3 weeks; sign removed after county or township health officer fumigated house.*
Where *was the disease caught?*	*On school bus from a carrier, "the Hinecker boy," who lived just ¹/₂ mile east of the family farm in central Iowa.*
Why *didn't the whole family get the disease?*	*Entire family received inoculation; all became ill. Arleyne's mother suffered most, but all were then immune.*
How *was the disease eliminated from the house?*	*Fumigation. Arleyne bundled up; family moved to basement, then to unheated upstairs, until house was declared safe.*
Extended Research Question: *What is the history of diptheria, and has it been eradicated?*	**Ideas for Research:** *Search GaleNet or EBSCO health databases; look in medical or general encyclopedias; search Web health sites such as CDC.*

©Academy School District 20, Colorado Springs, CO. Used with permission.

learned, and sharing their new understandings with a community of learners" (9). During the "My Family Artifact" lessons, students follow each step of Kuhlthau's information literacy model, scarcely recognizing that they are constructing their own understanding along the personal path of inquiry.

The Primary Source Librarian's Checklist:

❏ Reintroduce artifacts as primary sources by showing a slide show similar to **Figure 3.1** "Our Memories, Our Artifacts."

❏ Brainstorm artifacts that surround students in their daily lives. Use **Figure 3.2** "Exploring Our Artifacts" as a prompt.

❏ Take students on a visual tour of American Memory to show the depth and breadth of its primary source collections.

❏ Ask students to select an online artifact as a group, then model a practice analysis using the "Artifact Question Worksheet" in **Figure 3.3**. Discuss critical questioning skills as well as the importance of detail in historical writing.

❏ Discuss the significance of the "Extended Research Question" and what makes it researchable and also worthy of research. Give sample student questions and check for understanding by asking students to improve upon them.

❏ Hand out and discuss the **Figure 3.4** "Artifact Practice Activity" instructions.

❏ Ask students to print a copy of their selected artifact, attach it to a blank **Figure 3.3** "Artifact Question Worksheet," and complete the analysis.

❏ Conduct an interim assessment, using the **Figure 3.5** "Artifact Activity Checklist."

❏ Hand out the **Figure 3.6** "Family Artifact Final Project" instructions. Give students several days to bring their artifacts to school.

❏ Help students use a digital camera or a scanner to photograph or scan their artifact.

❏ Schedule classes for library research as they fill out the **Figure 3.7** "Family Artifact Questions" worksheet. In particular, help them write quality extended research questions.

❏ Use the diphtheria quarantine sign analysis in the **Figure 3.8** "Family Artifact Example" to model critical thinking skills and an actual analysis.

❏ Schedule time and equipment for students to assemble the final word-processed analysis.

❏ Evaluate student products using the **Figure 3.9** "Final Rubric—My Family Artifact."

❏ Find ways to display or feature student projects for teaching colleagues, parents, administrators, and other students through meetings, "best practices" sessions, conferences, newsletters, library displays, and other creative venues.

In the end, the young family historians carry home with them a newly-acquired family heirloom—the project itself—to share with grandparents, parents, aunts, uncles, and siblings. "My Family Artifact" now joins the family scrapbooks.

Figure 3.9: Final Rubric—"My Family Artifact" (page 1)

Final Rubric — "My Family Artifact"	Minimal 30 points each	Proficient 40 points each	Exemplary 50 points each
Artifact Worksheet, Selecting and Digitizing *Points earned =*	Selects artifact and can describe it to the teacher.	Selects artifact, asks another person (teacher, librarian, parent, other) to scan or take a digital photo of artifact and save.	Selects artifact, scans or takes a digital photo with minimal help, saves to disk or network.
Artifact Worksheet, Description *Points earned =*	Writes name of artifact.	Writes name of artifact plus short description and relationship to family.	Writes name of artifact plus description that gives evidence of the history of the artifact within family.
Who? What? When? Where? Why? How? Questions *Points earned =*	Simple, sometimes incomplete, lacking depth of inquiry.	Complete, specific, showing evidence of personal curiosity.	Complete, descriptive, requiring thoughtful answers.
Worksheet Answers *Points earned =*	Simple, sometimes incomplete, with mistakes in conventions.	Complete sentences (all answers), descriptive; answers match questions.	Complete sentences (all answers), descriptive nouns and adjectives; additional information shows evidence of interviewing and historical research.
Extended Research Question *Points earned =*	Simple Yes/No Question.	Question shows evidence of curiosity about artifact.	Question requires research into historical context of artifact.

Figure 3.9: Final Rubric—"My Family Artifact" (page 2)

Answers to Extended Research Question *Points earned =*	Student only asks family for answers; questionable accuracy.	Some evidence of research into historical period of artifact.	Ample evidence of research into historical context of artifact; cites more than one source.	
Final Word-Processed Document, Content & Writing *Points earned =*	Includes some information transferred from worksheet (description, relationship to family, questions, answers). Includes digitized artifact.	Includes complete description, relationship to family, and questions and answers from worksheet, minimum of errors in conventions, evidence of careful description and research. Includes digitized artifact.	Includes complete and grammatically correct description, relationship to family, and evidence of careful historical research so that it "teaches" history of the artifact. Includes digitized artifact.	
Final Word-Processed Document, Design *Points earned =*	Not organized for clear communication; uninteresting or confusing.	Visually attractive; design supports clear communication.	Grabs attention without distracting from message. Clearly organized and balanced, with elements thoughtfully placed and formatted for clear communication. Design fits theme of artifact.	
Total Points = */400*				

Chapter

4

Primary Source
Analysis Techniques

Information Literacy—The Heart of Primary Sources

From a librarian's perspective, information literacy lies at the heart of every effective lesson, including every primary source lesson. The library media specialist should never stray far from the American Association of School Librarians' publication, *Information Literacy Standards for Student Learning*, or from comparable state or local standards. In particular, the first three national standards, along with their "indicators," apply directly to primary source units. Other standards stress independent learning and social responsibility, such as crediting sources—all important pieces of primary source instruction and analysis.

Primary sources typically require students to explore ideas well beyond mere surface observations of the primary source itself. Questions always arise that invite further investigation. For example, a turn-of-the-century "Singer Souvenir" advertising card from the Smithsonian Institution that pictures New York City tourist landmarks leads students to learn both about the city of one hundred years ago and how the invention of the sewing machine changed women's lives. In another example, a careful reading of Abraham Lincoln's second inaugural speech ("With malice toward none..."), delivered near the end of the tragic struggle between North and South, leads to comparisons with his first inaugural speech delivered four years earlier under the cloud of approaching war. Now in the year 1865, "a weariness of spirit pervaded the nation" (White 109). How would Lincoln speak for an exhausted nation? How would he define the steps toward reconstruction and reconciliation? The speech leads learners to pose still more questions, and thoughtful questions lie at the heart of information literacy.

A student researching primary sources knows how to ask questions and where to find answers. As explained under Standard 1 of *Information Literacy Standards for Student Learning*, "The student knows when to seek information beyond his or her personal knowledge, how to frame questions that will lead to the appropriate information, and where to seek that information. The student knows how to structure a search across a variety of sources and formats to locate the best information to meet a particular need" (9). Several more detailed Standard 1 "indicators" apply to primary source questions:

Indicator 3: *Formulates questions based on information needs*. "Students change and refine their questions as their research proceeds by developing essential questions that go beyond simple fact-finding and that promote thoughtful interpretation, synthesis, and presentation of newly found knowledge."

Indicator 4: *Identifies a variety of potential sources of information*. "Students acquire strategies for locating a variety of formats to satisfy information needs, including print, nonprint, and electronic as well as human resources of varying points of view and depths of coverage, and they differentiate between primary and secondary sources."

Indicator 5: *Develops and uses successful strategies for locating information*. "Students quickly and effectively locate the most relevant information for research questions within the sources they have gathered, and they vary their strategies according to the format, organization, and search capability of the source and according to the particular issue they are researching."*

These indicators clearly match primary sources, but other information literacy standards apply equally well as students move from questions to research to knowledge to products. Along their research path, information literate students make their own decisions about organizing information from primary sources because no secondary source textbook writer has done it for them. Often, students must do preliminary research about the context of primary sources so that they can integrate the new knowledge with the old. They must also decide how best to present the new knowledge to their peers. At every step of the research process, they are applying multiple information literacy standards and indicators.

Finally, with every primary source experience, students strive toward the goal of becoming lifelong, independent learners. This goal is best expressed under Independent Learning Standard 6:

Students reflect on their own work and revise it based on feedback from others. They develop an intrinsic standard of excellence. They revise their information-searching strategies when appropriate. They also self-assess about their information-seeking process by asking themselves questions such as: Do my questions really get to the heart of what I need to know?

---

*From *Information Power: Building Partnerships for Learning* by American Association of School Librarians and Association for Educational Communications and Technology. Copyright © 1998 American Library Association and Association for Educational Communications and Technology. Reprinted by permission of the American Library Association.

and Have I found enough information to give an accurate picture of all sides of the issue? They approach research as a recursive process, revising the search as they answer their own assessment questions. They set their own criteria and check the quality of their own work. (*Information Literacy Standards for Student Learning* 30).

This non-linear, "recursive" process of investigation is pictured in **Figure 4.1** in a graphic that helps students visualize themselves using a process model to become "Information Literate Students."

Figure 4.1: Information Literate Students: A Process Model

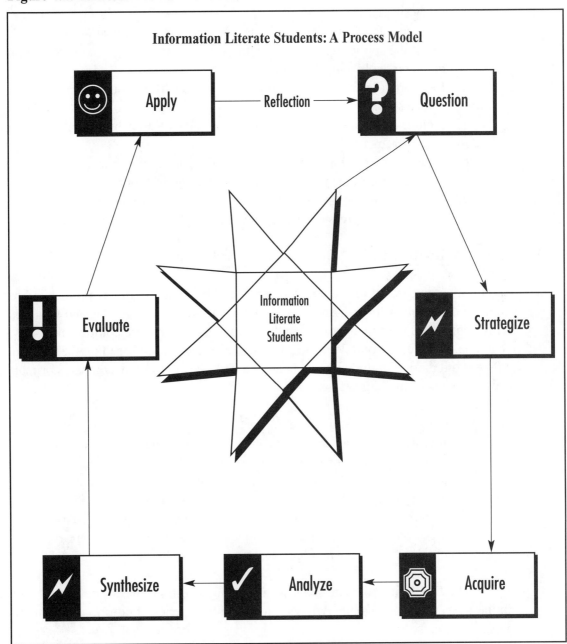

While this section has introduced the reader to the multiple information literacy standards that primary source lessons can meet, it only scratches the surface. When students work in groups, for instance, more "Social Responsibility Standards" (*Information Literacy Standards for Student Learning* 32–43) apply. Student researchers practice socially responsible information ethics when their teachers require proper bibliographic citations. They can also learn to detect and analyze bias and diversity of opinion in primary sources. The list continues.

By following the guidelines listed below, the library media specialist can form the habit of including information literacy standards in all primary source lessons:

1. Study diligently the American Library Association publication *Information Literacy Standards for Student Learning* or similar state or local information literacy standards.
2. Keep the standards handy in both print and electronic form.
3. Insert the applicable standards into every printed primary source lesson planned collaboratively with teachers.
4. Regularly discuss information literacy goals with teachers, administrators, and students.
5. Include information literacy standards alongside content standards in all evaluation instruments.
6. Consistently reinforce the vocabulary and concepts of information literacy while working with students both independently and in groups.
7. End every primary source lesson with a request for feedback from students about their progress toward the identified information literacy goals.

Finding a Framework for Primary Source Analysis

To reinforce the concept of primary sources, the "My Family Artifact" project in Chapter 3 relied on the simplest form of analysis — *who, what, when, where, why,* and *how* questions. Many approaches to primary source analysis exist, some far more complex than this simple technique. The "DoHistory" Web site, an interactive case study based on the remarkable 200-year-old diary of a midwife and healer named Martha Ballard, compares primary source analysis to a detective's investigation:

> The detective investigates a crime that was committed in the past. He looks for evidence such as fingerprints or witnesses or articles that link the suspect and the crime. Likewise the historian looks for evidence such as letters, diaries, court documents, objects used by the people being studied, and buildings where the people lived. After gathering evidence from primary sources, the historian creates a secondary source by writing about the findings, analyzing them, or putting them together into a story about the past." ("Using Primary Sources," par. 1).

The DoHistory Web site suggests answering a series of basic "detective" questions similar to those in "My Family Artifact," followed by a series of questions that pinpoint the *meaning* beneath them:

1. Why was this document/object written or made?
2. Who was the intended audience/user?
3. What questions does this source raise? What don't we know about this source?
4. What other information do we have about this document or object?
5. What other sources are like this one?
6. What other sources might help answer our questions about this one?
7. What else do we need to know in order to understand the evidence in this source?
8. What have others said about this or similar sources?
9. How does this source help me to answer my research question?
10. How does evidence from this source alter or fit into existing interpretations of the past?[1]

Researchers at the Center for Children and Technology, with support from the Kellogg Foundation, spent a year observing teachers and students using the Library of Congress American Memory collections of primary sources. They discovered that students profited most from unique analysis techniques developed for *each* category of primary source material:

> The teachers and students we observed had to develop new skills of observation and analysis with each of the media they used. With photos, they learned to take account of as many visual details as possible. With political cartoons, they began to attend to the symbolic use of imagery, making the task of interpreting historical cartoons something like cracking a code. For audio recordings such as political speeches, students noticed and discussed a speaker's use of vocal inflections and flourishes in addition to the words spoken. These different formal features were keys to getting the fullest historical insight from the document (Tally, par. 7).

In a perfect world, library media specialists and teachers would always find the time to customize instructions, questions, and assessments to fit every type of primary source, and that remains a worthy goal. In reality, generic primary source tools often fit the immediate needs of classroom teachers. The next section offers an all-purpose form that, while lacking customization value, does not compromise the intellectual integrity of the primary source analysis process. The form also places responsibility for making decisions throughout the analysis process firmly upon the student's shoulders, thus reinforcing principles of information literacy and independent learning.

A Five-Step Model of Primary Source Analysis

The "Primary Source Analysis Template" in **Figure 4.2** follows five steps and can be used with all types of primary sources. The explanations following correspond to each step in **Figure 4.2**. Based on a student-centered inquiry approach, the template builds toward successively higher levels of critical thinking.

[1] Used with permission.

Step 1: Internal Evidence. Through this preliminary observation exercise, students are forced to "confront two essential facts of historical work. First, the record of historical events reflects the personal, social, political, or economic views of the participants who created the sources. Second, students bring to the study of the sources their own biases, created by their own personal situations and the social environments in which they live" (*Teaching with Documents*, Vol. I, vii). In other words, the objective/subjective fields require students to distinguish between the biases of the primary source creators and the students' own tentative and possibly biased interpretations. Students often have difficulty distinguishing between fact and opinion, and they tend to make sweeping assumptions about emotions and intent. They need guidance to identify the dual subjective and objective natures of primary sources, as evidenced in a typical student observation of a pioneer photograph: "The settlers look sad because there are no trees." Teachers should not underestimate the time needed to model this basic fact versus opinion step.

Step 2: External Evidence. Often some type of bibliographic data accompanies primary sources, especially if they are located in museum or library collections or in other public or private archives. As students examine the bibliographic clues, they also ask themselves what evidence is missing. The latter is a far more difficult task than copying observable evidence. In spite of the difficulty, curiosity about unanswered questions and about subjective observations lead to Step 3, the most important part of the process.

Step 3: Research-based Evidence. The fragmentary internal and external evidence of the first two steps piques students' curiosity to continue their investigations. Based on the questions they create in Step 3, they will begin to fill in the blanks, effectively creating their own "captions" to accompany their primary sources. The depth and thoughtfulness of their questions will determine the overall success of the project as they begin to situate their primary sources in the proper historical and personal context. The library media specialist, along with the teacher, might step in at this point to lead students through Socratic questioning techniques that promote "synthesis of information into discernible categories of 'fact' and 'opinion'" (*Taxonomy of Socratic Questioning* 4).

Likewise, questions that progress through Bloom's Taxonomy (knowledge, comprehension, application, analysis, synthesis, and evaluation) build toward higher levels of student understanding ("Bloom"s Taxonomy: An AskERIC Response" 1). Hundreds of Web sites and print resources exist to help students and teachers become better questioners.

Across multiple primary source lessons, students will begin to recognize the levels of questions that incorporate complex thinking, leading to more reflective and challenging research. In an article entitled "Inquisitive Minds," writer John Barell tells a wonderful story about Isadore I. Rabi, a noted physicist who won the Nobel Prize for his work on electrons: "Mr. Rabi said that when he came home from school as a child, his mother did not ask him, 'So, what did you learn in school today?' Instead, she asked, 'Izzy, did you ask a good question today?' That difference—asking good questions—is what made him become a scientist, the Nobel laureate maintained" (46).

As they generate questions, students also identify strategies and sources to answer them, whether print, nonprint, online, or human. As in each step of the Primary Source Analysis Template, Step 3 can also be expanded for specific assignments. **Figure 4.3** on page 45, for

Figure 4.2: Primary Source Analysis Template (page 1)

Primary Source Analysis Template

	Objective Observations: (minimum of four)	**Subjective Observations:** (minimum of four)
Step 1: **Internal Evidence** "Information literate students question."*		
Step 2: **External Evidence** "Information literate students question."	**Objective Evidence:** (from bibliographic data)	**Missing Evidence:** (missing from bibliographic data)
Step 3: **Research-based Evidence** "Information literate students strategize, acquire, and analyze."	**Questions to Guide Research:**	**Search Strategies:** (resources and/or keywords)

Figure 4.2: Primary Source Analysis Template (page 2)

	Plan to Demonstrate Knowledge:	Outline of Main Points:
Step 4: **Synthesize Evidence and Research** "Information literate students synthesize."*		
Step 5: **Evaluate Product and Process** "Information literate students evaluate and apply."	Product Evaluation: (narrative)	Process Evaluation: (narrative)

***Key Belief: Schools and library programs empower students to become information literate.**

Through inquiry, students develop increasing levels of complexity in the following skills and abilities:
Question: Create essential questions about information needs.
Strategize: Develop plans for finding a variety of relevant information sources.
Acquire: Find information needed to answer questions.
Analyze: Evaluate sources, read content, refine and revise questions.
Synthesize: Learn by connecting information, experience, and prior knowledge.
Evaluate: Assess process and product.
Apply: Use knowledge ethically for the improvement of self and society.

* Adapted from "Guide to Libraries, Technology, and Learning" ©2002, Academy School District 20, Colorado Springs, CO. Used with permission.

Figure 4.3: Online Search Strategies Worksheet

Online Search Strategies Worksheet
Photographic Primary Source

Part I. Keyword Brainstorming Exercise

Research Question

Keyword 1		Keyword 2		Keyword 3
	AND		AND	
OR		OR		OR
	AND		AND	
OR		OR		OR
	AND		AND	

Part II. Search Terms

Write three potential Web searches below:

1. _____

2. _____

3. _____

Part III. Web Site Brainstorming Exercise

Circle the most useful and reliable categories for your research question.

History Web sites   Personal narratives or remembrances

Government Web sites   Subscription databases

Collections of historical photographs   Online encyclopedias

Class projects on the Web   Educational Web sites (.org or .edu)

Other _____

example, shows an "Online Search Strategies Worksheet" that helps students prepare an effective search for a *photographic* primary source analysis. Although online search strategies extend beyond the realm of this book, the worksheet serves as one example of the kind of expanded online learning opportunity available through primary sources.

Step 4: Synthesize Evidence and Research. Primary source research can end in an almost limitless array of products, and Step 4 is designed to give students some control over how they choose to demonstrate their new knowledge. In some cases, the teacher may assign a specific kind of presentation, but this step also encourages the teacher to match projects to individual learning styles and to differentiate instruction. **Figure 4.4**—"Presentation Ideas for Primary Sources"—shows a partial list of project options, limited only by imagination. The Step 4 template box labeled "Outline of Main Points" (**Figure 4.2**) helps students plan the product after they have decided how best to present their analysis.

Step 5: Evaluate Product and Process. When students continually self-evaluate, they become more capable, independent learners. Many of the project chapters throughout this book include assessment rubrics, but never at the expense of self-assessment. Step 5 in **Figure 4.2** provides a narrative space for students to write their thoughts about their own successes or failures and how they might change the process and product the next time they analyze a primary source.

Figure 4.4: Presentation Ideas for Primary Sources

Presentation Ideas for Primary Sources

1. Design a scrapbook of similar primary sources.

2. Make a photographic exhibition complete with explanatory signs.

3. Write a letter from one of the primary source characters to another.

4. Create a PowerPoint™ presentation using portions of the primary source.

5. Design a Web page to display the primary source analysis.

6. Memorize a famous speech and introduce it with the primary source analysis.

7. "Walk in the shoes" of the creator of the primary source by writing a narrative and playing the role of the creator.

8. Make a three-dimensional museum exhibit of the primary source. Label and explain.

9. Write and illustrate a children's book about the primary source.

10. Reenact a scene from the primary source.

"Letter From Gordon"—Example of a Primary Source Analysis

In an old family photograph album, a student discovers an intriguing photograph (**Figure 4.5**) of a woman standing beside a mailbox. She appears to be reading from a sheet of paper. The words "Letter from Gordon" are written at the bottom of the photograph, and that is all the student can fill in as objective evidence on the primary source analysis worksheet.

Figure 4.5: Letter from Gordon

Figure 4.6: Gordon with Mother

Figure 4.7: Gordon on crutches

One week later the student has learned that the woman in the photo was her great grandmother, and "Gordon" is her great uncle, now 84 years old and living in an Iowa nursing home. As a result of a more thorough perusal of the photograph album (**Figures 4.6** and **4.7** show further photographic evidence), combined with personal interviews, she has answered many questions about Gordon's role in World War II, the severe wounds he suffered in the Battle of the Bulge, his family's experiences on the home front, and his eventual recovery and return to his family.

The student was now able to fill out the customized "Online Search Strategies Worksheet" introduced in **Figure 4.3** and now pictured in the "Completed Online Search Strategies Worksheet" in **Figure 4.8** on page 48, selecting keywords, combining them as search terms, and circling the best Web site categories for research before going online.

To research the question—"How did soldiers communicate with their families during World War II?"—the student also checked out several book collections of GI letters from the public library, as well as the PBS American Experience series video, "The War Letters." The "Completed Primary Source Analysis" in **Figure 4.9** on pages 49 and 50 shows the process from beginning to end, from the first objective observations to the actual research process, and finally to the honest evaluation narrative.

Completed Online Search Strategies Worksheet
Photographic Primary Source

Part I. Keyword Brainstorming Exercise

Research Question
How did soldiers communicate with their families during World War II?

Keyword 1		Keyword 2		Keyword 3
soldier(s) or GI(s)	AND	*correspondence*	AND	*home*
OR		OR		OR
World War II	AND	*letters*	AND	*"home front"*
OR		OR		OR
"World War II soldiers"	AND	*v-mail*	AND	*family or families*

Part II. Search Terms

Write three potential Web searches below:

1. *"World War II soldiers" AND letters AND famil**

2. *GI AND v-mail AND "home front"*

3. *"World War II" +correspondence +soldiers*

Part III. Web Site Brainstorming Exercise

Circle the most useful and reliable categories for your research question.

(History Web sites)   (Personal narratives or remembrances)

(Government Web sites)   Subscription databases

Collections of historical photographs   Online encyclopedias

Class projects on the Web   (Educational Web sites (.org or .edu))

Other _____

Figure 4.9: Completed Primary Source Analysis (page 1)

Completed Primary Source Analysis

	Objective Observations: (minimum of four)	Subjective Observations: (minimum of four)
Step 1: **Internal Evidence** "Information literate students question."*	1. Photo has "Letter from Gordon" written on bottom edge. 2. A woman wearing a dress is standing beside a mailbox, and she is reading from a sheet of paper. 3. There is a building in the background. 4. The mailbox stands beside a dirt or gravel road.	1. The woman was excited to find the letter in her mailbox because she opened it and read it immediately. 2. The mailbox was not in a town. 3. The woman's house is in the background. 4. The woman is "Gordon's" mother.
	Objective Evidence: (from bibliographic data)	**Missing Evidence:** (missing from bibliographic data)
Step 2: **External Evidence** "Information literate students question."	No "bibliographic data." Other clues: 1. The photo is in a family album, with surrounding photos dated 1941–1944. 2. Surrounding photos include many labeled "Gordon," and he is often in a military uniform. 3. One later photo shows Gordon on crutches and without one leg.	1. The woman is not identified. 2. It is not known where the letter was written from or from where it was mailed. 3. Location of mailbox unknown. 4. Photo is not dated.
	Questions to Guide Research:	**Search Strategies:** (resources and/or keywords)
Step 3: **Research-based Evidence** "Information literate students strategize, acquire, and analyze."	1. Who owns the album? What can they tell us about the photo and the surrounding photos? 2. How did soldiers communicate with families during World War II? 3. Who was Gordon and what was he doing when he wrote the letter? 4. Were soldiers allowed to write home about anything they chose? 5. Is it possible to find letters written by World War II soldiers?	1. Interview Gordon or other family members. 2. Follow up interviews with research about the WWII time period, home front experiences, what military campaigns Gordon might have experienced, etc. 3. Keyword ideas: World War II, home front, correspondence, letters home. 4. Look for actual World War II GI letters.

Figure 4.9: Completed Primary Source Analysis (page 2)

	Plan to Demonstrate Knowledge:	**Outline of Main Points:**
Step 4: **Synthesize Evidence and Research** "Information literate students synthesize."	*Ideas to consider (1st choice underscored):* 1. *One-page explanatory letter and oral presentation.* 2. *Reenactment of photograph, reading the letter aloud that Gordon might have written.* 3. *Multimedia presentation with scanned photograph.* 4. *Write the letter that Gordon may have written. Include details from research.*	1. *Gordon enlisted in the U.S. Army in 1942 and took his basic training in Florida.* 2. *Gordon's mother is pictured reading a letter from him, probably written from Florida training, in front of her Iowa farmhouse.* 3. *Because of censors, Gordon would not have written details of his battle experiences in Europe. Base writing on actual letters from GIs.* 4. *Gordon was wounded during the Battle of the Bulge.*
Step 5: **Evaluate Product and Process** "Information literate students evaluate and apply."	**Product Evaluation:** (narrative) *I learned a lot about my Great Uncle Gordon's World War II experiences from my interview with him. My grandmother told me wonderful stories about what it was like at home in Iowa and about how much the family looked forward to Gordon's letters. I tried to write the kind of letter that I read in several books of collected V-mail from GIs. I should have written an introduction to explain more before I read the letter, and I could have practiced more.*	**Process Evaluation:** (narrative) *It helped a lot to do the keyword exercise before I did online research, but I was frustrated because there weren't many letters available online. I had better luck finding books of soldiers' letters. The interviews with Gordon and my grandmother (Gordon's sister) were the best part. I was surprised to learn about censorship of V-mail, and even though I learned a lot about World War II, I couldn't put it in the letter. I liked the way a simple photo started this project.*

*Key Belief: Schools and library programs empower students to become information literate.

Through inquiry, students develop increasing levels of complexity in the following skills and abilities:

Question: Create essential questions about information needs.

Strategize: Develop plans for finding a variety of relevant information sources.

Acquire: Find information needed to answer questions.

Analyze: Evaluate sources, read content, refine and revise questions.

Synthesize: Learn by connecting information, experience, and prior knowledge.

Evaluate: Assess process and product.

Apply: Use knowledge ethically for the improvement of self and society.

* Adapted from "Guide to Libraries, Technology, and Learning" ©2002, Academy School District 20, Colorado Springs, CO. Used with permission.

Customizing Primary Source Lessons

As previously discussed, students need to develop skills that match each of the media studied, and as library media specialists experience each new primary source category, they can begin to customize the lessons. The Bank Street College of Education, working in collaboration with staff at the Center for Improved Engineering and Science Education (CIESE), has developed an excellent introduction to four types of primary sources. Called "Historical Treasure Chests," the project provides questions that guide the investigation of a *photograph* named "Milliner's Daughter," a *letter* from Theodore Roosevelt, Sr. to his young son, a sixteenth-century Spanish *map* of the Americas, and a rare *book* entitled *The Juvenile National Calendar* from 1825. The lists of questions not only frame each type of primary source investigation, they also model questions specific to that particular photograph, letter, map, and rare book.

Many teachers, already skilled at guiding students through written texts, miss the rich teaching potential of visual sources. The creative teacher, however, uses the fragmentary and often disconnected evidence from visual images such as photographs, films, art works, posters, and cartoons to help students build historical understanding. To guide students as they interrogate visual sources, teachers can draw from the customized list of "Questions for Visual Primary Sources" in **Figure 4.10**. If all students analyze the same image, the library media specialist and teacher can easily add specific questions or rewrite the questions in **Figure 4.10** to fit the image studied. It is always wise to model the process beginning with a single representative image.

Figure 4.10: Questions for Visual Primary Sources

Questions for Visual Primary Sources

1. Spend at least five minutes observing every possible detail of the image. What do you see? Whom do you see?

2. What objects, visual styles, design elements, or technology help you identify the time period?

3. Does the creator of the image appear to have personal experience with the content?

4. Who created the image and why?

5. Who is the intended audience?

6. What does the image tell us about the person (or group) that made it?

7. Does the image express a point of view or a bias, either subtle or obvious?

8. If the visual source accompanies a text, how does it help the text communicate its message?

Film and television productions pose special challenges to visual analysis, but these moving image "documents" absolutely contribute to the historical primary source record. As bandwidth and transmission speeds increase and streaming video becomes more widespread in schools, students and teachers gain access to historical film and television accounts of history. From the early films of Thomas G. Edison viewable online from the American Memory *Inventing Entertainment* collection to current broadcast news, students must develop the critical viewing skills to analyze moving images, including the ability to recognize bias and to distinguish between factual reporting and editorial interpretation. In the book *Image as Artifact: The Historical Analysis of Film and Television*, editor John O'Connor states, " ... the researcher who ignores the close study of moving image evidence has failed to cover the subject; and the number of these areas is sure to increase in the future" (1).

Students can still use the majority of visual primary source questions above to analyze film and television content. The first step still requires that the viewer examine the source closely, in this case by viewing it repeatedly. In addition, critical viewers "must consider the nature of visual communication, learning at least some of the technical terminology used to characterize the elements of a motion picture shot and the types of editing devices available to the filmmaker" (O'Connor 17). The more students know about the elements of a shot and the editing techniques of filmmakers, the more critically they can evaluate the moving picture sources.

Likewise, audio sources such as speeches and folksongs require special "reading" skills. For example, students examine elements of intonation, delivery, and technology of the world's famous speeches to understand their emotional and historical impact. As with visual sources, they need to spend time "observing" the audio files, listening for quality, voice, emotion, intent, stylistic elements, and evidence of the technology used. If bibliographic data is available, students can identify speakers or performers, places, time periods, and audiences. As always, objective and subjective observations lead to further research. Sometimes recordings also combine with visual resources such as printed sheet music or long-playing record jackets, which become part of the evidence for analysis.

When students approach *textual* analysis of primary source documents, the library media specialist and cooperating teacher can draw from numerous online lists of questions about written documents. One such list is reprinted in **Figure 4.11**, "Questions for Textual Primary Sources." The textual analysis questions correspond strikingly with the visual analysis techniques already listed. The questions again focus on identifying bias or intent as well as the meaning within the historical context of the times.

A final important point: it should be noted that students often face language obstacles to understanding historical *texts*. In particular, archaic language and difficult vocabulary can stand in the way of understanding historical diaries, letters, broadsides, essays, and more. Teachers should always include some kind of vocabulary study as part of textual analysis: "Preparation for reading should focus on the readability of text, broadly considered. With vocabulary, familiar concepts may be signified by unfamiliar and archaic words. Previewing such vocabulary and providing more contemporary synonyms may be helpful" (Afflerbach and Van Sledright, 705). In addition, students might not recognize early forms of handwriting without pre-instruction and practice. Students need formal instruction to offset the frustration of both archaic language and early penmanship. The DoHistory Web site cited earlier in this chapter includes java applets that help students read eighteenth-century handwriting through a "magic lens" as they transcribe the difficult words and spellings of Martha Ballard's diary.

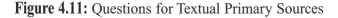

Figure 4.11: Questions for Textual Primary Sources

Questions for Textual Primary Sources

1. Who wrote the document?

2. Who was the intended audience?

3. What is the story line?

4. Why was the document written?

5. What type of document is this, or what is its purpose?

6. What are the basic assumptions made by the author?

7. Can I believe this document?

8. What can I learn about the society or person that produced this document?

9. What does this document mean to me?

   —Charles T. Evans. "Principles of Historical Document Analysis." Used with permission.

The Primary Source Librarian in Action

When students experience primary source lessons, they question, strategize, acquire, analyze, synthesize, evaluate, and apply at increasing levels of complexity. To lead them systematically through primary source inquiries, the primary source librarian can refer to the list of tested tactics below.

The Primary Source Librarian's Checklist:

☐ Study the information literacy standards (pages 47–51) as well as the process pictured in **Figure 4.1**.

☐ Study the DoHistory Web site as a metaphor for primary source detective work.

☐ Research unique analysis techniques for each category of primary source material.

☐ Study and test with students the five-step process of primary source analysis using the template in **Figure 4.2**.

☐ Use primary source lessons to improve online search techniques by utilizing the strategies worksheet in **Figure 4.3**.

☐ Differentiate primary source instruction by encouraging students to try a variety of presentation ideas (**Figure 4.4**).

☐ Use the complete primary source analysis of "Letter from Gordon" (**Figures 4.5–4.9**) to model an analysis for students.

☐ Study or use with students the "Historical Treasure Chests" Web site to increase understanding of different types of primary source materials and analyses.

☐ Use the "Questions for Visual Primary Sources" in **Figure 4.10** or the "Questions for Textual Primary Sources" in **Figure 4.11**, as well as the discussion of film and audio sources to customize primary source lessons according to type.

☐ Research ways to overcome some of the barriers to understanding archaic handwriting and language.

☐ Share the many primary source worksheets, lists, and forms with colleagues, particularly those willing to take a risk to develop a primary source inquiry.

The huge variety of primary source materials makes the exercise of developing analysis techniques both exciting and daunting, but ultimately rewarding for students, teachers, and library media specialists. As Levy writes, "Documents have much to teach us, I believe, if we will only listen" (6). Library media specialists can lead the "listening."

Chapter

5

A School-Wide Patriotic Speech Festival

Teaching Democratic Ideals Through Historic Speeches

Generations of American students have been molded by a vision for teaching democratic ideals that has existed since the first public schools opened in the mid-1800s. In their study of a century of public school reform, professors David Tyack and Larry Cuban concluded, "At its best, debate over purpose in public education has been a continuous process of creating and reshaping a democratic institution that, in turn, helped to create a democratic society" (142). Each succeeding generation of educators has continued to prepare its students to participate responsibly in civic life and to understand the basic principles that guide a constitutional democracy.

In these first troubled years of the twenty-first century, Americans find themselves reexamining and reaffirming the democratic principles set down in the Constitution of the United States as well as in other historic documents, and once again they are calling for schools to renew their commitment to teaching those principles to the next generation. Dorothy Sisk, a leader in gifted education, writes, "In our schools, we have an opportunity to link democracy, power to the people, equity, and literacy instruction" (24). She believes that by studying the words of great leaders for democracy throughout history, students will also begin to "grasp the importance of literacy and the power of the word" (25).

Through the "Patriotic Speech Festival" presented in detail in this chapter, students memorize and perform some of the most influential speeches, documents, and poems in American history. An excellent example of the interdisciplinary potential of primary sources, this unit helps students meet standards in civics, history, English/ language arts, and drama. A team of library media specialists, teachers, classified staff, administrators, parents, and community members facilitates and shares in this remarkable celebration of democratic ideals. Together, they are continuing the long tradition of teaching values central to a democratic way of life.

Competition Selections—Patriotic Speech Festival

The Founding of a Nation

Henry, Patrick	Give Me Liberty or Give Me Death
Jefferson, Thomas	First Inaugural Address
Paine, Thomas	Common Sense
Tecumseh	To Governor Harrison at Vincennes
Thoreau, Henry David	Civil Disobedience
Washington, George	To the American Troops
Washington, George	Farewell Address

Forming a National Identity

Anthony, Susan B.	Are Women Persons?
Douglass, Frederick	What Is Your Fourth of July to Me?
Joseph, Chief	I Will Fight No More Forever
Lincoln, Abraham	The Gettysburg Address
Mott, Lucretia	The Anti-Slavery Society
Seattle, Chief	The White Man Will Never Be Alone
Stanton, Elizabeth Cady	The Male Element
Truth, Sojourner	I Want Women to Have Their Rights

A Vision of Twentieth-Century America

Angelou, Maya	On the Pulse of Morning
Jordan, Barbara	We Can Form a National Community
Johnson, Lyndon Baines	The Great Society
Kennedy, John F.	Ask Not What Your Country Can Do for You
King, Jr., Martin Luther	Nobel Prize for Peace Acceptance Speech
King, Jr., Martin Luther	I Have a Dream
MacArthur, Douglas	Duty-Honor-Country
Roosevelt, Theodore	The Duties of American Citizenship
Whittaker, Otto	I Am the Nation
Wilson, Woodrow	Americanism and the Foreign Born

Challenges of the Twentieth Century

Carter, Jimmy	Farewell Address
Chisholm, Shirley	The Business of America Is War
DuBois, W.E.B.	Advice to a Schoolgirl
Goodno, Barbara	American Women in the Military
Hughes, Langston	Let America Be America Again
Kennedy, John F.	Special Message to Congress on Urgent National Needs
Kennedy, John F.	A Call for Justice
Laviera, Tato	AmeRícan
Roosevelt, Eleanor	The Great Common Hope
Roosevelt, Franklin Delano	War Address to the Congress

An Overview of the Patriotic Speech Festival

The Patriotic Speech Festival has continued to grow and gain attention since its unpretentious beginnings five years ago at Eagleview Middle School in Colorado Springs, Colorado. Today every eighth grade student (370 in all) selects a historic speech, document, or poem from a list of thirty-eight "Competition Selections" (**Figure 5.1**) that has been divided into four chronological and conceptual stages of American history: "The Founding of a Nation," "Forming a National Identity," "A Vision of Twentieth Century America," and "Challenges of the Twentieth Century."

The works represent men, women, minorities, famous leaders, and lesser-known but equally inspiring authors and orators. They range from extremely difficult, lengthy selections to simpler, shorter, but still challenging pieces that meet the differentiated learning needs of the entire population of eighth graders. As any editor discovers when making selections to include in an anthology, the choices naturally mirror the biases and experiences of the editor, and so it is with this list. The works in **Figure 5.1** do reflect, however, a number of changes made over the years to respond to student preferences and to give balance and pizzazz to the final public program. For example, students have found that short poems limit their dramatic range compared to some of the more powerful speeches, so event coordinators have moved most of the poetry to a category called "Exhibition Pieces" (**Figure 5.2**). During the final competition, students or groups of students present the non-competitive exhibition pieces to fill the times when judges are consulting or tallying their votes.

The list can be revised and simplified for elementary students or made more challenging for high school students. The library media specialist can support revisions by identifying additional famous speeches from readily-available print and electronic resources, some of which are referenced throughout this chapter. Once the students have made their

Figure 5.2: Exhibition Pieces

Exhibition Pieces	
Author	**Title**
Anonymous	I Am Your Flag
Congress	Preamble to the Constitution of the United States
Congress—Thomas Jefferson, Principal Author	Introduction and Preamble to the Declaration of Independence
Congress	The Bill of Rights
Emerson, Ralph Waldo	Concord Hymn
Finch, Francis Miles	The Blue and the Gray
Hughes, Langston	Democracy
Lazarus, Emma	The New Colossus
Lindsay, Rachel	Abraham Lincoln Walks at Midnight
MacLeish, Archibald	The Land of the Free
Paine, Thomas	Liberty Tree
Seattle, Chief	The Earth Is Precious
Turner, Nancy Byrd	They Will Look for a Few Words
Whitman, Walt	I Hear America Singing

selections, they have a number of options for research to increase their understanding of the historical time period, the context of the speech, and biographies of the orators or authors.

Students memorize their selections, then practice and present them within their classrooms before their teachers and peers, who evaluate their performances and pass on a list of semi-finalists to the festival coordinator. Outside judges come in for the semi-final round, which is held in the library or another performance space. The final competition takes place in the evening before an audience of parents and families, honored guests, teachers, judges, and members of the media.

School Days, School Days, Good Old Golden Rule Days

Students might be surprised to discover that their grandparents and great-grandparents often memorized famous American speeches and poems as a part of their lessons in rhetoric and elocution. In his study of curriculum in American classrooms from 1890–1980, Larry Cuban found evidence that school officials and teachers at the turn of the century shared a belief from the "infant science of educational psychology that … children learned best through repetition and memorization" (31). In a young adult book entitled *Don't Whistle in School: The History of America's Public Schools*, Ruth Tenzer Feldman writes, "By the early twentieth century … [students] had elocution lessons—complete with a system of dramatic gestures—to learn to be effective public speakers" (44). Still closer to the theme of this chapter, Kathleen Kennedy Manzo writes in her history of curriculum throughout the twentieth century, "Patriotism was another popular theme of many early mandates" (par. 45).

To help students make connections between historical precedent and the upcoming memorization exercise, the library media specialist can facilitate two exploratory primary source activities in a computer lab or from a single computer with a projection system in a library or classroom. The first activity looks at a nineteenth-century book from "Making of America," a thematic online collection that draws on primary sources from the University of Michigan and Cornell University, collaborators since 1995 on "a digital library of primary sources in American social history from the antebellum period through reconstruction" (par. 1). The 1831 book by Samuel Woodworth is grandly named *Melodies, duets, trios, songs, and ballads, pastoral, amatory, sentimental, patriotic, religious, and miscellaneous. Together with metrical epistles, tales and recitations*. It is filled with the types of recitation pieces that American children memorized half a century after the founding of our nation. Students can simply browse the myriad selections, pausing along the way to read them aloud and to wonder about the emotional language of the period. Even better, they can search for patriotic pieces as practice or exhibition pieces for the Patriotic Speech Festival. A typical nineteenth-century patriotic verse from the Woodworth book, rather flowery by today's standards, reads as follows:

> We here assemble to rejoice
> That patriots, with united voice,
> Once rose and made this manly choice,
> For them and their descendants.
> They freedom's eagle raised on high—
> Freedom's eagle—freedom's eagle—

They freedom's eagle raised on high,
And swore to fight and bravely die,
If foreign despots dare deny
Columbia's Independence. (127)

The second activity takes students to the American Memory Web site <http://memory.loc.gov> to search for actual accounts of early school life. One of the best narrative sources is the "American Life Histories" collection, where students can do a key-word search on *recitation* or related terms to find personal remembrances of elocution contests, debates, spelldowns, and declamations. For example, they can read about Nebraskan C. P. Wiltse, who "took a great deal of interest in national politics" and was "a great admirer of McKinley" (Form B). In 1939 he recalled that as an adult he became secretary of a literary lyceum, a club of civic-minded citizens that met to debate issues of the day and to listen to recitations and musical numbers. "I cannot recall the recitations, but we had some excellent elocutionists in those days," Wiltse reported (5).

Also in 1939, Elam Franklin Dempsey of Georgia, son of Narcissa America Smith, recalled putting on debates during vacation time after having learned techniques of debate in school. "And it did us good, too. That old time custom contributed to civic thinking, and taught us to think on our feet and get up before the public and put our thoughts into words. I've noticed that those who excelled at those things have done well in life since then," Dempsey said (3).

Students might question if they need to transfer old-fashioned beliefs about public speaking and civic participation to their education today. Does memorization have a place in today's schools, or will students dismiss it as mere busy work? What can students learn from the words and ideas of the great orators? Debating these questions will help students think critically about the coming assignment.

Introducing Patriotic Speeches

Before students can move forward with their dramatic presentations, they need to understand the role that rhetoric—or skillful use of language—can play in changing listeners' views or in moving audiences to action. As educator Peter A. Gilbert states so well, "It is not great ideas alone that move people's hearts and minds, but great ideas eloquently expressed" (5). He goes on to justify the study of famous speeches: "Students may become more discriminating citizens if they can understand not only how great language works but also how manipulative language works. Such understanding should help them distinguish the saccharine from the tender, the sentimental from the heartfelt, the thoughtless from the thoughtful, the demagogue from the leader, even—dare I say it—falsehood from truth" (12).

One of the most effective ways to introduce historic American speeches comes from a set of activities developed by the U. S. National Archives and Records Administration (NARA) in a two-volume set, *Teaching with Documents: Using Primary Sources from the National Archives*. Educators can also access many of the activities online through NARA's "Digital Classroom" (http://www.archives.gov). One lesson takes students through a written document analysis of Franklin D. Roosevelt's first typed draft of the speech he delivered to Congress and to the nation via radio the day following the Japanese bombing of Pearl

Harbor—the famous "A Date Which Will Live in Infamy" speech. Students can follow a series of steps to analyze copies of the draft, which President Roosevelt revised extensively in his own handwriting. First they define vocabulary terms such as *infamy*, *premeditated*, *onslaught*, and *dastardly*. Secondly, they identify "techniques for enhancing the effect of a speech: repetition, alliteration, emotionally charged words, appeal to self-preservation, and assurance of moral superiority" (164) in the address. They also consider whether Roosevelt's handwritten changes enhanced or weakened the address in terms of the intended audience.

Students can listen to the actual speech from sound files on the NARA Web site while completing a "Sound Recording Analysis Worksheet" found on the Web site that includes pre-listening, listening, and post-listening questions. Two extended activities developed by NARA enhance student investigative skills: (1) a comparison of Roosevelt's address with Patrick Henry's "Liberty or Death" speech, and (2) a set of interview questions for students to ask of older adults who actually heard Roosevelt deliver his radio address.

Certainly other famous speeches and documents can be used to introduce the writing and presentation techniques that make a speech great. For older students, the introduction and preamble to the "Declaration of Independence" provide excellent material for analysis, as does the "Bill of Rights" section of the United States Constitution. Again, the National Archives and Records Administration Web site offers excellent teaching materials linked from their Exhibit Hall section featuring "The Charters of Freedom." Linked from the Web site, a particularly helpful article by Stephen E. Lucas, "The Stylistic Artistry of the Declaration of Independence," appears custom-made for high school students preparing for document-based questions in their Advanced Placement United States History classes. Students learn that in Thomas Jefferson's famous preamble:

> Each word is chosen and placed to achieve maximum impact. Each clause is indispensable to the progression of thought. Each sentence is carefully constructed internally and in relation to what precedes and follows. In its ability to compress complex ideas into a brief, clear statement, the preamble is a paradigm of eighteenth-century Enlightenment prose style, in which purity, simplicity, directness, precision, and, above all, perspicuity were the highest rhetorical and literary virtues. One word follows another with complete inevitability of sound and meaning. Not one word can be moved or replaced without disrupting the balance and harmony of the entire preamble. (par. 13)

The Bill of Rights, another document in "The Charters of Freedom" exhibit, is linked to another excellent background article that students can use to follow the writing and revisions from draft to final form. Entitled "A More Perfect Union," the article by Roger A. Bruns describes the ratification process and the compromises that led to the final draft following a series of eloquent speakers who tried to influence the outcome.

Connecting Great Speeches with Great Speaking Skills

Eloquence. Presence. Emotion. Few speeches pass the tests of greatness if delivered with mediocrity, and students need to understand the interplay between the language itself and the delivery. Former White House speech writer and linguist William Safire introduces his 1997 book, *Lend Me Your Ears: Great Speeches in History*, with a written speech of his own about what makes a great speech. (Safire's book is also an excellent source of speeches for the Patriotic Speech Festival.) He outlines ten steps to a great speech in a balanced blend of writing elements and speaking techniques. William Safire's essay will prompt students to identify characteristics of strong and weak speeches and apply the learning to their own speeches. For example, after Safire discusses structure, he adds, "A skeleton needs life. Beyond structure is pulse. A good speech has a beat, a changing rhythm, a sense of movement that gets the audience tapping its mind's foot" (21). He emphasizes the need to practice and to have a *reason* for giving a speech. He urges readers to avoid "the dread disease of dribbling-off" (27) at the end of a speech, a problem common among inexperienced student speakers.

The "Speech Analysis Form" in **Figure 5.3** on page 62 will guide students to a better understanding of the written elements that strengthen their own selections and that they can exploit as they prepare their own high-impact deliveries. Although some questions on the worksheet can be completed based on careful study of the speech itself, others will require the resources of the library media program. The historical questions help students analyze the themes and the times of the speeches through library research. Without an understanding of historical context, student performances will almost certainly be flat and dispassionate—in short, boring.

The library media specialist, always intent on connecting students to resources, would be remiss not to take advantage of the many *human* resources available for helping students develop their speaking skills. The following list points out numerous ways that the library media specialist can support students long before they reach the final patriotic speech competition:

- Schedule the library for a workshop on memorization and presentation skills by the school's drama teacher or the speech and debate coach.
- If there is a Toastmasters organization in the community, invite members to present a workshop or to work individually with students.
- Invite older students active in forensics programs to work with younger students.
- Invite winners from previous years' competitions to model techniques by returning to present their winning pieces.
- Invite parents and school or community volunteers to participate in student practices.
- Instruct volunteers to reinforce the importance of eye contact, volume, pacing, articulation, gestures, body language, and other details that strengthen a performance.
- Encourage volunteers to watch for bad body habits such as slouching, putting hands in pockets, swaying, and playing with jewelry, as well as equally distracting vocal behaviors such as excessive use of "um" or "uh," sniffling, and so on.

As students begin practicing their speeches, they should receive the evaluation forms to be used later by judges. Five criteria will be rated: memorization, interpretation, verbal delivery, non-verbal delivery, and audience response. Based on feedback from judges, a

Figure 5.3: Speech Analysis Form

Speech Analysis Form

Title of Speech:	Speaker/Author:

What is the general theme of the speech?	List three specific points made in the speech.
	1.
	2.
	3.

What is the historical context of the speech?	List three events chronologically (with dates) that relate to the historical context of the speech.
	1.
	2.
	3.

What is the speaker/author's point of view or relationship to the speech?	List three reasons why the speaker/author might have given or written this speech.
	1.
	2.
	3.

Does the speaker make a persuasive argument?	Place a check before the literary devices or elements that you identified in the speech.
Yes	❏ strong invitation to listen
No	❏ alliteration
Not sure	❏ imagery
	❏ exaggeration
	❏ metaphor
	❏ repetition (parallelism)
	❏ rhythm
	❏ memorable phrases
	❏ strong peroration (conclusion)
	❏ clear organization
	❏ clear purpose

three-stage rubric with the categories "Needs Improvement," "Developing," and "Advanced" works more effectively than an overly detailed assessment that interferes with attending to the speeches. Using the official "Judge's Form" in **Figure 5.4** on page 64, students can rate themselves and each other during practice sessions as they gain experience in the techniques of public speaking.

Activities and Extensions

The Patriotic Speech Festival can generate numerous interdisciplinary learning activities that enhance historical and linguistic understandings of the speeches. Each of the ideas outlined briefly in this section can be used to differentiate instruction, but each idea also has the potential to grow into a lengthy lesson plan in itself.

To begin, gifted and talented students can use library and Internet resources to complete a scavenger hunt that matches one of the four historical categories. Sample questions from "The Founding of a Nation" category, for example, might ask gifted students to explain the difference between a Patriot and a Loyalist or to discover where Henry David Thoreau spent the night to avoid paying taxes to support the Mexican War.

English teachers might ask the students to write a five-paragraph essay based on their answers to the speech analysis activity (**Figure 5.3**). The analysis leads quite naturally to the five-paragraph essay format because of its split into three points that support the theme, three historical events related to the speech, and three reasons for giving the speech. The library media specialist can furnish Web sites that teach the five-paragraph essay format by searching one of dozens of lesson plan megasites such as *Blue Web'n*, *KidsClick!*, and *Kathy Schrock's Guide for Educators*. Teachers can access "The Five-Paragraph Essay," a comprehensive, award-winning writing tutorial, at <http://www.geocities.com/SoHo/Atrium/1437/>.

One inquiry technique that can be used with higher-level thinkers begins with a handout of a patriotic speech or poem stripped of its speaker, writer, and title. Students use clues from the work itself to investigate the time period, the issues discussed, vocabulary, style, and audience before hypothesizing about the missing information.

The Patriotic Speech Festival also provides rich potential for biography study. Extending expectations beyond basic biography research, the library media specialist can help students develop online search strategies to locate primary sources related to their speaker. The primary sources might include photographs, presidential documents, newspaper reviews of the speeches, and even music of the speech's time period.

Finally, if time allows, a set of activities on the American Memory Learning Page leads students through the collection entitled *American Leaders Speak: Recordings from World War I and the 1920 Election*. This collection "contains fifty-nine sound recordings of speeches by American leaders [including] the seldom heard voices of Calvin Coolidge, John D. Rockefeller, Jr., Samuel Gompers, Henry Cabot Lodge, and John J. Pershing" (par. 1). Critical thinking activities range from historical comprehension to historical issue analysis and decision making. The arts and humanities activities ask students to examine persuasive speaking, context clues, creative writing, speaking and listening skills, and significant themes. These activities are linked from the "American Leaders Speak" home page as Learning Page "Collection Connections."

Figure 5.4: Judge's Form

Judge's Form

CATEGORY	NEEDS IMPROVEMENT	0–5 PTS	DEVELOPING	6–8 PTS	ADVANCED	9–10 PTS
MEMORIZATION	Stumbles or pauses often; dependent on prompting.		Mostly memorized; some stumbling or prompting.		Flawlessly memorized.	
INTERPRETATION	A. Presentation fails to convey meaning, content, or theme. B. Just memorized words with little emotional connection to piece.		A. Meaning, intent, and theme mostly clear. B. Emotional content, mood, characterization sometimes inconsistent with piece.		A. Meaning, intent, and theme clearly interpreted. B. Emotional content, mood, characterization clearly interpreted.	
VERBAL DELIVERY	A. Pronunciation indicates lack of understanding; mumbled diction. B. Little evidence of using pacing, voice quality, or pitch to emphasize meaning. C. Difficult to hear; introduction not forceful; ending "dribbles off."		A. Most words pronounced clearly; diction somewhat inconsistent. B. Pacing, voice quality, and pitch usually emphasize important parts. C. Somewhat inconsistent volume; voice does not always engage listeners.		A. Words pronounced clearly; excellent diction. B. Pacing, voice quality, and pitch used to communicate important parts effectively. C. Excellent volume, introduction and conclusion forcefully presented.	
NON-VERBAL DELIVERY	A. Delivery detracts from message (looking down, fidgeting, giggling). B. Little or no eye contact. C. Gestures and facial expressions, if any, inconsistent with message.		A. Delivery generally confident; may be hesitant or unsure in poise and posture. B. Generally good eye contact. C. Gestures and facial expressions mostly consistent with message.		A. Delivery is natural, confident; excellent poise and posture. B. Excellent eye contact. C. Gestures and facial expressions strongly consistent with message.	
AUDIENCE RESPONSE	Audience shows confusion or lack of interest.		Audience generally polite, engaged.		Audience is engaged, responsive, and enthusiastic.	
	Column Points=		**Column Points=**		**Column Points=**	

NAME OF STUDENT   TITLE OF SELECTION   TOTAL POINTS   /100

NAME OF JUDGE

While it is important to recognize that no single school could possibly accomplish all of the extended learning activities proposed above, there is nevertheless ample room for creativity and customization of learning from famous speeches. Some of these activities can lead to a full-blown "Patriotic Speech Festival," but library media specialists and teachers need to recognize that it is sometimes wise to start small and build toward the level of a school-wide or a district-wide festival.

A Community Celebration

In no case is the devil more in the details than when an entire community participates in an evening school event, so it is essential that a Patriotic Speech Festival coordinator be appointed. The coordinator handles the following lengthy list of arrangements to guarantee the festival's success:

- Selects date of semifinals and finals for the school's master schedule.
- Produces and/or revises teacher and student notebooks of speeches, rules, activities.
- Meets with all participating language arts and social studies teachers to discuss timeline and responsibilities.
- Attends parent and community meetings to gain support and provide information.
- Solicits donations of prizes and cash support.
- Arranges for judges for semifinals and finals.
- Sends letters, criteria, and judging packets along with speeches and exhibition pieces to judges.
- Schedules rooms for semifinals.
- Collaborates with library media specialist on workshops and research activities.
- Sends flyers to school board members, veteran groups, etc.
- Organizes breakfast and training for semifinals judges.
- Produces a program for the final competition (best done on patriotic specialty paper).
- Works with custodians to arrange and decorate the space for finals.
- Writes script for the Master of Ceremonies.
- Arranges dinner and training for finals judges.
- Schedules winning speech demos for School Board as well as parent and veteran groups.
- Sends thank you notes.
- Plans an evaluation meeting and records suggestions.

The long list above implies an even longer list of minutiae: t-shirts, advertising, decorations, videotaping, donation storage, copying, color coding ballots by category, nametags, tips for judges, pencils, flowers, labeled seats for honored guests, water pitchers and glasses, ushers and greeters, sound systems, patriotic stationery, and so much more. It is understandable that one of the essential budget items covers a one-day substitute teacher for the coordinator, but obviously large groups of willing volunteers must also work hard to produce a successful event. The library media specialist can help at every turn, from collaborating for research to handling some of the numerous organizational details.

The Patriotic Speech Festival opens far-reaching public relations opportunities for schools, beginning with the make-up of the finals judging team: local and state board of education members, school district administrators, professors of English and Speech, city council members, active military, military retirees, World War II veterans, former POW-MIAs or Medal of Honor recipients, community activists, and police and fire fighters—in short, people who are held in high regard by the community.

The final competition opens in a festive atmosphere with a student singing or playing the national anthem. Four finalists compete in each of the four categories as a rarely-needed prompter sits nearby. Between categories, students individually and in groups perform exhibition pieces while judges and helpers tally the results. Students in the English Language Learners program perform perhaps one of the most moving exhibition pieces— a poem or the lyrics of a patriotic song translated and pieced together in their various native languages. The evening culminates in an awards ceremony in which the winner of each category receives a United States savings bond.

Thus ends one of the most inspirational performances of the school year. Principal Ross MacAskill wrote in his weekly bulletin, "This week, one of the more remarkable events in the life of our school occurs: the Eighth Grade Patriotic Speech Festival. It is remarkable for several reasons:

- ◎ It is one of those things of which every eighth grader has been a part. Oh, there are other things—Colorado Student Assessment Program (CSAP), 6-Trait Writing, falling in love, but this one is ours.
- ◎ It shows the tremendous talent of our kids. Although only sixteen kids make the finals, another dozen could have easily done so.
- ◎ It is a celebration of patriotism, oratory, history, confidence, dramatic and emotional appeal, and a job well done.
- ◎ It is those finalists rising on the shoulders of their 370 classmates who began the journey a month ago.
- ◎ It is a public example of the positive results of your colleagues.
- ◎ It is … remarkable." (1)

The Primary Source Librarian in Action

As stated in the *National Standards for History*, "Worthy inquiries are especially likely to develop if the documents students encounter are rich with the voices of people caught up in the event and sufficiently diverse to bring alive to students the interests, beliefs, and concerns of people with differing backgrounds and opposing viewpoints on the event" (Overview, par. 1). At every pivotal period in American history, great orators have come forth to deliver speeches that move individuals to action. The Patriotic Speech Festival gives a sense of the sweep of history and of the influence of those great orators.

The Patriotic Speech Festival offers multiple opportunities for interdisciplinary learning, and it meets a wide range of content standards in social studies, civics, history, English, and performing arts. Long after the final celebration, the speeches will echo in students' ears, just as they have echoed across centuries of the American experience. The library media specialist participates at every stage of the festival by co-teaching, providing resources, connecting people, and supporting both organizers and students throughout the competition.

The Primary Source Librarian's Checklist:

- ☐ Introduce historical precedents of recitation in schools.
- ☐ Help students discover examples of recitation in early schools.
- ☐ Provide teaching materials that introduce famous speeches (from the National Archives and Records Administration, for instance).
- ☐ Provide "Competition Selections" (**Figure 5.1**) and "Exhibition Pieces" (**Figure 5.2**).
- ☐ Provide "Speech Analysis Form" (**Figure 5.3**) and facilitate its use.
- ☐ Help students research the historical context of the speeches and biographies of speakers.
- ☐ Collaborate with teachers on lesson extensions (scavenger hunt by category, "stripped" speeches, five-paragraph essays, "American Leaders Speak" recordings, etc.).
- ☐ Locate additional speeches or poems as needed.
- ☐ Offer to coordinate public speaking workshops.
- ☐ Arrange to have former contestants perform and advise.
- ☐ Volunteer to handle some of the detailed arrangements.
- ☐ Offer to serve as a judge of preliminary competitions or as an advisor.
- ☐ Connect contest organizers with community members to serve as judges.
- ☐ Provide the "Judge's Form" (**Figure 5.4**).
- ☐ Always attend the final competition, and write congratulatory notes to participants.

In the end, the many professional educators who have worked so diligently to plan the final grand event can join the students who have worked equally hard, the judges, and the parents and supporters in the audience in a celebration of patriotism and learning. From primary sources to passionate performances, students build an appreciation of the most powerful words of history: "Let your imagination carry you beyond the words on the page so that you can hear the music of the speaker's delivery—the pitch of the voice, the inflection, the cadence, the changing rhythm, the alliteration, the pulse, the sense of movement—and most of all, the passion that stirred the heart of an audience and left an indelible mark on history" (Goodwin, xxiii).

Chapter

6

Collecting Letters, Connecting Learning

Letters — Primary Source Treasures for Every Age

Of all the primary sources that enrich student learning, perhaps the humble letter creates the most extensive array of learning possibilities. For years, literary-minded intellectuals have decried the slow demise of correspondence, but letters from the past continue to connect students of today to every historical era and every curricular area, from history to science to literature. A single letter, no matter how famous or how ordinary the letter writer or recipient, can spark a student investigation that personalizes the human experience far more than any secondary source. As Kenneth Rendell of the University of Oklahoma states in his book on collecting historical letters:

> Letters and documents are the most direct link we can have to the heroes
> and heroines, villains, and ordinary people of the past. They show these
> men and women as human beings, dealing with matters on a scale that all
> of us can relate to. We begin to appreciate that their lives may not be all
> that different from our own — that people of the past confronted the same
> feelings and fears that we all do, that they persevered to achieve the
> goals — both great and small — of their lives (1).

Because letters hold so much promise for creative teacher/library media specialist collaborations across grade levels and curricular areas, it is impossible to cover in a single chapter the myriad research directions letters can take. For that reason, this chapter offers a foundation for using letters as primary sources in the curriculum but relies on the library media specialist to remain aware of opportunities specific to each school setting.

The first part of the chapter takes a decidedly literary bent, with a project that begins with "epistolary fiction" (a novel written in the form of a series of letters), but ends with a turn toward research in science and conservation. Moving from fictional letters to a more traditional analysis of actual historical letters, students need to be aware of special problems in letter analysis such as archaic vocabulary and difficult syntax. A complete hands-on historical letter project reinforces the techniques introduced in Chapter 4 while adding specialized letter analysis techniques to the library media specialist's primary source bag of tricks. Finally, an original letter writing project helps students synthesize research based on primary source letters. Letter writing is NOT dead!

Epistolary Fiction As a Starting Point

Letters have long played a role in literature. Whether an author sprinkles a novel with letters as a literary device or engages in regular personal correspondence, letters have often influenced the writing act as well as the writer's own life. Scholars who specialize in Ralph Waldo Emerson, Emily Dickinson, or Edna St. Vincent Millay learn from their personal correspondence as well as from their literary works.

The specific genre of "epistolary fiction" represents a powerful way to introduce letters as primary sources because students connect letters to the idea of story. Several familiar novels written in the form of a series of letters match reading and comprehension levels of 4th to 12th grade students, and they cover a surprisingly wide range of themes and historical eras. Thus teachers of reading, literature, history, current issues, and even science can use these novels to bring important concepts to life. The Web site of the Madison Public Library has an extensive annotated list of "Epistolary Fiction" to consider at <http://www.scls.lib.wi.us/madison/booklists/epistolary.html>. The following annotated list of epistolary works gives an idea of the range available to librarians and teachers of 4th through 12th grade students:

- ◎ **4th–8th Grade.** *Pioneer Girl*, by Maryanne Caswell. Not a novel, but a series of authentic letters written by 14-year-old Maryanne Caswell to her grandmother in 1887 as her family moved from Palmerston, Ontario to homestead on the Canadian prairie. First published in 1952, *Pioneer Girl* richly describes chores, planting, caring for livestock, building a sod house, and much more to help students understand the pioneer experience.
- ◎ **4th–8th Grade.** *Letters from Rifka*, by Karen Hesse. In letters to her cousin, a young Jewish girl named Rifka writes of her family's flight from Russia and from persecution in 1919. She must remain in Belgium while her family emigrates to America. An easy-to-read introduction to the immigrant experience.
- ◎ **6th–8th Grade.** *Feeling Sorry for Celia*, by Jaclyn Moriarty. A light but engaging coming-of-age novel appropriate for middle level readers. Themes of imperfect parents, teen-age angst, suicide, and romance told in letters and notes. Can be used to teach voice and characterization.
- ◎ **6th–8th Grade.** *Last Days of Summer*, by Steve Kluger. A coming-of-age tale about a Brooklyn boy in the early 1940s and his hero, a New York Giants third baseman. A funny and poignant story told through "primary sources" that include letters, postcards, box scores, news clippings, report cards, matchbook covers, telegrams, and even dispatches from President Franklin D. Roosevelt.

- **6th–12th Grade.** *Ella Minnow Pea*, by Mark Dunn. The citizens of the fictional island of Nollop resist encroaching totalitarianism in this delightful epistolary fable. A word lover's dream, and also an excellent choice for Banned Books Week discussions.
- **8th–12th Grade.** *Alice's Tulips*, by Sandra Dallas. This novel of the Civil War home front is comprised of letters written by the capricious 18-year-old Alice to her sister over the three-year period during which her new husband serves as a Union soldier. Alice matures as she deals with wartime deprivations, a stern mother-in-law, and gossip in a closed community.
- **8th–12th Grade.** *Letters to Callie: Jack Wade's Story*, by Dawn Miller. Set in 1864, this sequel to *The Journal of Callie Wade* is told partly in the form of letters to Jack Wade's sister. More than a western romance, this book helps students understand the dark, perilous side of the pioneer experience.
- **10th–12th Grade.** *The Color Purple*, by Alice Walker. A Pulitzer Prize-winning novel told through the letters of Celie, a poor and barely literate African American woman living in the South. Celie struggles to escape her cruel, degrading treatment by the men in her family and town. A controversial, powerful epistolary novel for mature students.

Additional epistolary novels to consider:

4th–6th Grade	Beverly Cleary	*Dear Mr. Henshaw*
6th–8th Grade	Nick Bantock	*Griffin & Sabine trilogy*
6th–8th Grade	Maureen Sappey	*Letters from Vinnie*
8th–12th Grade	Mary Myers	*Dear Ellen Bee*
7th–12th Grade	C. S. Lewis	*The Screwtape Letters*
8th–12th Grade	Helene Hanff	*84 Charing Cross Road*
8th–12th Grade	Mary Shelley	*Frankenstein*
9th–12th Grade	Joanne Greenberg	*Where the Road Goes*
10th–12th Grade	Elizabeth Hailey	*A Woman of Independent Means*
10th–12th Grade	Barry Unsworth	*Pascali's Island*

From Epistolary Fiction to Primary Sources—An Example

In her 1999 novel, *Letters from Yellowstone*, Diane Smith used correspondence to tell the tale of an 1899 scientific expedition to Yellowstone. Throughout the book, a colorful cast of characters recounts its misadventures and successes via letters. The mild-mannered botany professor, Howard Merriam, writes detailed and regular letters to his mother. His expedition is joined by a pithy agriculturalist, Dr. Andrew Rutherford, who halfheartedly intends to look for plants that can be cultivated. Added to the mix are two undergraduate students, a Chinese cook, a Crow Indian who is an expert on traditional uses of plants, and a surprising last-minute replacement member, A. E. Bartram, a medical student with a passion for botany. A. (Alexandria) E. Bartram turns out to be an attractive and capable female, which throws the expedition into turmoil, prompting Professor Merriam to write home, "Dear Mother, what am I to do with a woman? We already have a cook" (27).

Students quickly find themselves caught up in this story, hardly realizing that they are learning about national park history, the westward movement, exploration, naturalist studies, and even the trials of early women scientists to gain recognition and respect. The book stands on its own as a fine example of young adult epistolary fiction, but the next step—adding research through online primary sources—solidifies, extends, and enriches student understanding far beyond the novel. A simple search on *Yellowstone* at the Library of Congress's American Memory Web site attests to the wealth of primary source materials just waiting for students to discover them. Students can pursue dozens of lines of inquiry based on *Letters from Yellowstone*.

To begin, the *Yellowstone* search brings students to *The Evolution of the Conservation Movement, 1850–1920*, an American Memory collection that documents early efforts to conserve America's natural heritage. For example, students can read the 1872 congressional "Act to set apart a certain Tract of land lying near the Head-waters of the Yellowstone as a public Park" that established Yellowstone National Park, Wyoming, as the first national park in the history of the nation and of the world. They can read President Theodore Roosevelt's goals of forest conservation and preservation as well as John Muir's *Our National Parks*, an influential and beautifully-written portrait of some of the nation's great scenic wildernesses.

For an art and visual literacy connection, the library media specialist or cooperating teacher can project an 1875 Thomas Moran chromolithograph of the "Hot Springs of Gardiner's River, Yellowstone" from the same conservation collection. In addition, students can view actual film footage of some of the first tourists to Yellowstone National Park from the American Memory collection entitled *Inventing Entertainment: The Motion Pictures and Sound Recordings of the Edison Companies*. This 1899 Edison film (the same year in which the Diane Smith novel takes place) shows double-decker coaches drawn by six horses, crowded on top and inside with tourists waving hats and handkerchiefs as they pass.

To build map skills, students can compare early survey and tourist maps of Yellowstone from the American Memory *Mapping the National Parks* collection with modern tourist maps available from the National Parks Service Web site. They will also enjoy zooming in on portions of the park explored by characters in the novel. As a culminating project, students might produce their own 1899 tourist brochures by combining their favorite maps and images with the knowledge they have gained from written and visual records of park development as well as from the novel.

Perhaps the primary source document with the most potential to make the novel real for students can be found in an 1876 report from *The Nineteenth Century in Print* online collection jointly developed by American Memory and the University of Michigan. Students will be amazed by the similarities to the novel as they read William Ludlow's United States Army Corps of Engineers *Report of a reconnaissance from Carroll, Montana territory, on the upper Missouri, to the Yellowstone national park, and return, made in the summer of 1875*. Following the general report by Ludlow, the document includes a special zoological report, a geological report, and even a description of newly-discovered fossils. Students could not ask for a more authentic primary source to match the epistolary novel set in 1899.

Beginning Letter Analysis

Just as fictional letters and edited collections of authentic letters in book form can lead to hundreds more discoveries, so can single letters from other eras deepen student understanding through research. Library media specialists and teachers can build curriculum around individual letters based on a theme such as poverty, war, immigration, work, or environmentalism. Likewise, they can teach historical periods through letters—the decades of the twentieth century, for example, or the Great Depression, the Vietnam War, or the Jazz Age. Still other letters represent the common thoughts and experiences of women, minority groups, writers, and artists. In other words, letters can humanize a wide variety of topics and times. No matter who has penned the letter, "Letters give us 'a better understanding of life' because they provide us with immediate and often striking insight into human nature and the human experience" (Carroll, xlii).

Students trained in the primary source analysis techniques of Chapter 4 (**Figure 4.2**, page 43) will have little difficulty applying similar techniques to letter analysis. Using the template as a guide, they make objective and subjective observations from the text, then generate questions to ask of the text as well as search strategies to follow where their curiosity leads them. In an effort to enhance this generic template, the library media specialist may choose to reinforce the guide in **Figure 4.2** by designing a graphic organizer or simple worksheet more specific to letters as primary sources. The "Letter Analysis" template in **Figure 6.1** can be used for all grade levels and periods of letters studied, or it can be fine-tuned on short notice to fit an assignment more closely.

Throughout this book, readers will return again and again to the importance of asking questions of each primary source. Even though students develop their powers of observation through basic primary source analysis, they will reach higher levels of thinking only when they follow leads based on their own questions. Thus, the objective observations required by the first page of the **Figure 6.1** "Letter Analysis" lead to the far deeper inquiry required by the content and guided research questions of the second page.

While completing the second half of the "Letter Analysis" worksheet, students make decisions about both the intent and the content of the letter. They begin to situate events and descriptions in the larger historical context. They search for meaning in obscure and difficult words. Most of all, they set the stage for in-depth research through their own "researchable" questions, thinking ahead to strategies for research within the available pool of resources. This is information literacy at its best.

The Challenges of Letter Analysis

For a variety of reasons, letters, like any historical primary source texts, pose specific problems for student readers. First, the vocabulary in letters from another era may be archaic or at the least slightly old-fashioned. Students today hardly use words such as *whiffletree*, *neuralgia*, or *middling*! The difficult or unfamiliar words in many letters from the past help students build critical reading skills that require both a dictionary and an ability to utilize contextual clues.

An entertaining way to introduce letters from the past to older students is to read sample letters from old etiquette manuals. One such treatise, rather ostentatiously titled *The lady's guide to perfect gentility, in manners, dress, and conversation... also a useful instructor in letter writing*, is part of the American Memory collection, *An American Ballroom Companion—Dance Instruction Manuals Ca. 1490–1920*. It was so popular that it was reissued ten times between 1857 and 1890. Its author warns letter writers of the time that "Correct spelling and good grammar are so essential to fine writing that the absence of them destroys the force of the best sentiments" (Thornwell 158). Students will enjoy interpreting the model letter of "a lady in answer to a letter in which her suitor intimates his wish to discontinue acquaintance" (158). The letter concludes as follows:

> But deem me not so devoid of proper pride as to wish you to revoke your
> determination, from which I will not attempt to dissuade you, whether you
> may have made it in cool deliberation, or in precipitate haste. Sir, I shall
> endeavor to banish you from my affections, as readily and completely as
> you have banished me; and all that I shall now require from you is this, that
> you will return to me whatever letters you may have of mine, and which I
> may have written under a foolish confidence in your attachment, and when
> you were accredited as the future husband of,
> Sir,
> Yours as may be,
> HENRIETTA ALLSTON (167)

Once students conquer the vocabulary, they still face the challenge of complicated syntax and formal letter format. The student who normally signs off an e-mail with "C-ya" or "TTFN" (Ta ta for now) may find quite incomprehensible the following closing from the etiquette guide: "I am, honored madam, your obliged niece, Fannie Hall" (182).

Penmanship and punctuation (or the lack of it), too, can make old letters difficult to read, but the library media specialist can turn this challenge into a decoding exercise. How was the letter *r* written in the year 1905? Did the writer use correct spelling? Are words written in elaborate Spencerian script or a more crudely rendered script? Do capital letters occur in unexpected places? Students may find a magnifying glass useful, particularly as they transcribe old letters by means of their own handwriting or a computer keyboard. Transcription exercises force students to read and observe closely and provide them with a more readable format for further research.

Perhaps the greatest challenge to understanding letters is the student's own lack of life experience. It is important to remember that most students today have experienced only the 1990s and early 2000s firsthand. The 1990–1991 Persian Gulf War is as unfamiliar to them as the Civil War. Old letters filled with references to unknown places and events as well as daily tasks remain completely foreign to a twelve-year-old or an eighteen-year-old.

Selecting Letters for Analysis

Whereas thousands of letters worthy of study can be located online, others reside in personal, family, and local museum and library collections. The most effective letters come from the students themselves, and the library media specialist and cooperating teacher can begin a letter unit by asking students to bring in examples from their families. With the permission of their parents, students might share family letters from the Vietnam War era or even

Figure 6.1: Letter Analysis (page 1)

Letter Analysis

Name of Student _____

CATEGORY	ANALYSIS
Source 1. Write the name of the online collection (with URL), book, or owner of the letter. 2. Describe the collection (if information is available).	1. 2.
Physical Description 1. Describe the condition and materials used in the letter (type of paper, condition and color of paper, letterhead, water damage or wear, fading, folding, envelope, stamps, etc.). 2. Describe the physical writing (ink or typescript, color, legibility, spaces and margins, penmanship).	1. 2.
General Letter Format 1. Date of letter 2. Name of letter writer 3. Person(s) to whom letter was written 4. Address of person(s) receiving letter (if available) 5. Where letter was written 6. Salutation (greeting) 7. Closing	1. 2. 3. 4. 5. 6. 7.

Figure 6.1: Letter Analysis (page 2)

CATEGORY	ANALYSIS

Content
1. Why was the letter written?
 	
2. In your opinion, what were the three most important points that the writer included in the letter?
 	
3. List other events, personal information or concerns, requests made, and other details given by the writer.
 	
4. What was the educational level of the writer? How do you know?
 	
5. What was the relationship of the writer to the recipient? How do you know?
	1.
	
	2. •
	
	   •
	
	   •
	
	3. •
	
	   •
	
	   •
	
	4.
	
	5.

Vocabulary List at least 4 unfamiliar words from the letter.	1. 2. 3. 4.
Guided Research—Object 1. Write one unanswered but "researchable" question about the object itself (physical format, stamps, condition, etc.)	1.
Guided Research—Content 1. Write at least four "researchable" questions that the letter leaves unanswered (themes, personal details, events, living conditions, historical context, etc.).	1. 2. 3. 4.

Mom's college letters to home in the 1980s. To safeguard precious family letters, the library media specialist or the students themselves can scan them, print the scanned image, and return the originals to the safekeeping of the family.

For those teachers who wish to concentrate on a single historical period, there are numerous published collections available, both print and online. Letters written by famous people join a growing number of letters written by ordinary citizens. Editor Thomas Dublin states in a collection of women textile mill workers' letters from the mid-1800s, "Increasingly, historians are becoming aware of the need to expand our vision of history to incorporate the experiences of the not-so-famous Americans who have until now found scant place in the story of our nation's past" (2).

To support the study of letters as primary sources, the library media specialist must always be attuned to the curriculum. Which historical periods do fifth graders cover? What discoveries in chemistry might have been accompanied by correspondence? How would an authentic letter enhance the study of literature? Whether the library media specialist locates one significant letter or many, and whether letters become the focus of a unit or simply a lesson introduction or extension, the library media specialist performs a valuable service by collecting materials that support the curriculum. A core collection of letters includes both books and online resources, and the library media specialist makes that collection readily available to collaborative partners in a variety of curricular areas.

A Sample Exercise in Letter Analysis

The following analysis activity began with the discovery of a single letter in a bundle of old family letters. It illustrates the potential for building both knowledge of a time period and information literacy skills based on questioning primary sources. Written by G. Boone to his wife, Sarah E. Boone, the letter dates from the American Civil War. It is pictured with its envelope and archivist tools in **Figure 6.2** on page 78, "Letter from G. Boone."

To begin the activities based on the G. Boone letter, the library media specialist or teacher distributes copies of the front and back of the letter along with copies of the envelope to all students. Several "props" lend more authenticity to the exercise — copying the letter on yellowed or stressed paper of the original size and weight, asking students to cut and fold the envelope to its original size, even providing the white gloves and magnifying glasses that are the tools of an archivist. The students then examine the letter and envelope, making preliminary observations of the physical object, the handwriting, the stamps, the address, and the letter format.

Before asking the students to transcribe the letter, most teachers will want to give some background on letters from the Civil War period. Many of the hundreds of American Civil War Web sites include letters as well as explanations of common themes. The "Valley of the Shadow" Web site <http://www.iath.virginia.edu/vshadow2/>, one of the most moving and complete Civil War Web sites, includes letters written by common soldiers from both the North and the South. Describing the themes of soldiers' letters, it states, "Most frequently, soldiers seemed to write about home; wondering about particular people as well as general events. Their letters often seemed to be an effort to reconnect with home, to hold on to the familiarity of home in the time of war they were experiencing. They wrote about love, local politics, agriculture, old friends, and other ideas that were connected with home" (par. 1).

An excellent print source for background on Civil War soldier letters is an educational kit called "Civil War: A Simulation of Civilian and Soldier Life during the American Civil War, 1861–1865," by Terry Handy and Bill Lacey. A "Letters Home" activity in this role-playing collection states that "Salutations almost always began: 'My dear and effectionat [sic] wife' or something very close. Next, the soldiers gave a report on their health…. Following this would be inquiries or comments on affairs at home" (22). The activity goes on to discuss penmanship, spelling, and grammar. It ends with a list of key words and phrases that appear in letters from the war years, including *strawfoot, muster out,* and *skeddadle.*

After discussing general themes of Civil War soldier letters, students set to work transcribing the actual letter, either on a computer as shown below or in their own handwriting.

After leading a discussion of first impressions and preliminary observations about the content of the letter, the library media specialist and teacher distribute the "Letter Analysis" worksheet (**Figure 6.1**). Students complete the worksheet, paying special attention to the last two sections of questions that will later guide their research. The "Boone Letter Analysis" in **Figure 6.3** on pages 81 and 82 shows a sample worksheet completed by students.

Ideally, students will have access to the Internet after their questions have been approved as relevant and researchable, although they can find answers to general questions about a Civil War soldier's life in many print resources. While the questions on the completed worksheet hardly exhaust the possibilities, especially given a letter the length of G. Boone's, they set the course for some exacting, curiosity-driven research. Following is a sampling of student Internet discoveries based on their questions:

Fort Pocahontas   Augt 28th 1864

Dear wife

      We are still here waiting anxiously to be relieved. we got orders yesterday to cook 4 Days rations saying that our relief would be here this Evening. but It has not yet come and there is no certainty when they will come. we have had the promise of being relieved Several times & always have been disapointed. but I hope It will not be very long for we are all very anxious to get home as our time was up on the 19th of this month I am well I hope thee is the same for health is one great blessing.

It is not very pleasant to be unwell so far from home. we are about thirteen hundred miles from home now. when we get to Washington Capt. G. W. Gibbs said he would telegraph to Salem when we would be there or when we expected to be there. I suppose you was all a looking for us last Sunday. but in vain I only wish that It had been so.

For I know how It is to be disapointed. especially here. I wish I was at home to take a good meal with thee as I know I could enjoy It. we have had some Roasting ears. also apples & peaches. there is a goodeal of fruit in this country. but the only way to get It is to get It by forageing. which is not so very desirable a way to get It. If a person has got money they can get along pretty well. but otherwise It is pretty hard, to be in the army. give my respects to all inquiring friends. I suppose G. Street will be ready to go to Philadelphia before I get home. how are they all getting along by this time. I suppose the draft will come off on the 5th of next month but we hear that the money has been raised to free Perry Township. I think we have done our share to be out so long for the benefit of others.

Continue to write & direct to washington to follow the regiment untill we leave Washington. If thee has any change send me a little at a time so that there will not be much of a risk.

So Farewell Dear Wife   G. Boone

- A "George Boone" served on the Union side with the 143rd Ohio Infantry National Guard ("ONG" on the envelope), Company D, as a Sergeant. This information was originally compiled by Frederick Dyer, who had been a drummer boy during the Civil War. In 1905, Dyer began five years of work on the "Compendium of the War of the Rebellion" based on thousands of Union soldier index cards (U. S. National Park Service Civil War Soldiers and Sailors System).

- The 143rd Regiment did duty in the trenches at Bermuda Hundred, City Point and Fort Pocahontas until August 29, the day after Boone wrote his letter. They were "mustered out" September 13, 1864. Thirty-two men were lost during service, all by disease (Civil War Archive Union Regimental Histories Ohio).

- The "Old Point Comfort, VA" postmark was stamped on mail from soldiers of the Union Army of the Potomac. Old Point Comfort was located just north of Norfolk across Hampton Roads, the site of the duel between the Monitor and the Merrimac. It remained in Union hands throughout the war. Unpaid letters were sent with a due cover, as the "Due 3" indicates on the envelope (Kimbrough).

- Fort Pocahontas, located 16 miles west of Williamsburg, Virginia, was a supply depot made famous in 1864 by a victory of the United States Colored Troops over Major General Fitzhugh Lee, Robert E. Lee's nephew. Today it is being excavated and restored by archeologists and students of William and Mary College. The site is owned by the grandson of the 10th U. S. President, John Tyler. <http://www.fortpocahontas.org>

Given reliable Internet connections and essential training in Internet search strategies, student sleuths find themselves quickly hooked on authentic historical research. The thrill of this hunt began with an obscure Civil War soldier's letter, but it ended with new understandings and a growing ability to "formulate historical questions from encounters with historical documents" and to "obtain historical data from a variety of sources" (*National Standards for History*, Historical Thinking Standard 4).

Certainly, other lesson options can lead to meaningful historical research through letters. For example, this lesson could have connected to Sandra Dallas's book, *Alice's Tulips*, an epistolary novel of the Civil War. Taking another approach, the library media specialist and cooperating teacher could have located hundreds of equally moving soldiers' letters, enough to distribute a different letter to each student. With foresight and creativity, the library media specialist and teacher team can transform student learning into exciting inquiry from the starting point of a simple letter.

A Culminating Epistolary Activity

From reading epistolary fiction to conducting historical inquiry to … writing? Yes, the epistolary emphasis of this chapter connects all three skills if taken one step further to include actual letter writing activities. Students who write letters from a historical character's point of view, whether fictional or real, demonstrate a deeper level of understanding of eras and events. The goal is to synthesize disconnected bits of research into convincing, student-produced letters.

For letter writing activities to culminate the Civil War letter lesson above, the library media specialist need look no further than the classroom activities link on the Public

Boone Letter Analysis

Name of Student _____

CATEGORY	ANALYSIS
Source 1. Write the name of the online collection (with URL), book, or owner of the letter. 2. Describe the collection (if information is available).	1. *Family collection of author.* 2. *Bundle of family letters from Boones and Coffees, mostly from early 1900s.*
Physical Description 1. Describe the condition and materials used in the letter (type of paper, condition and color of paper, letterhead, water damage or wear, fading, folding, envelope, stamps, etc.). 2. Describe the physical writing (ink or typescript, color, legibility, spaces and margins, penmanship).	1. *Heavy buff-colored paper in good condition, folded two times, U.S. Sanitary Commission in fancy script on letterhead, 4-1/2 X 7-1/2 inches, yellow-colored envelope, "Soldiers Letter Wm Hastings Chaplain 143 Regt O N G" written on left side of envelope, "Due 3" stamped upper right envelope, round stamp with AUG 30 in center and Old Point Comfort VA around it.* 2. *Written in pencil, fairly easy to read, one page front and back filled with writing, almost no margins or spaces, good penmanship, some letters hard to read.*
General Letter Format 1. Date of letter 2. Name of letter writer 3. Person(s) to whom letter was written 4. Address of person(s) receiving letter (if available) 5. Where letter was written 6. Salutation (greeting) 7. Closing	1. *August 28, 1864* 2. *G. Boone* 3. *Sarah E. Boone* 4. *Salem Columbiana Co Ohio* 5. *Fort Pocahontas* 6. *Dear wife* 7. *So Farewell Dear Wife*

CATEGORY	ANALYSIS

Content
1. Why was the letter written?
 	
2. In your opinion, what were the three most important points that the writer included in the letter?
 	
3. List other events, personal information or concerns, requests made, and other details given by the writer.
 	
4. What was the educational level of the writer? How do you know?
 	
5. What was the relationship of the writer to the recipient? How do you know?
	1. *To let Sarah know when George might come home.*
	
	2. • *Why George hasn't come home yet.*
	
	  • *To expect a telegram about coming home.*
	
	  • *Send money.*
	
	3. • *Time was up on Aug. 19, and it is already Aug. 28.*
	
	  • *Food is hard to get except by "forageing."*
	
	  • *Perry Township has paid to get out of the draft.*
	
	4. *Fairly high. Good vocabulary, well organized, mostly good grammar (except for confusing or missing punctuation).*
	
	5. *He is her husband. He calls her "thee" and "dear wife."*

Vocabulary List at least 4 unfamiliar words from the letter.	1. *Roasting ears* 2. *goodeal* 3. *forageing* 4. *inquiring friends*
Guided Research—Object 1. Write one unanswered but "researchable" question about the object itself (physical format, stamps, condition, etc.)	1. *What is "Old Point Comfort" stamped on the outside of the envelope?*
Guided Research—Content 1. Write at least four "researchable" questions that the letter leaves unanswered (themes, personal details, events, living conditions, historical context, etc.).	1. *Where is Fort Pocahontas?* 2. *What does "143 Regt ONG" mean?* 3. *What did soldiers eat and how did they get their food?* 4. *Were soldiers drafted into the Union and Confederate armies?*

Broadcasting System (http://www.pbs.org) Web site. Joan Brodsky Schur has written an eight-day unit plan based on American Civil War letters to accompany the well-known Ken Burns *The Civil War* documentary series. "The lesson begins with an analysis of what historians can learn from ordinary Americans whose Civil War letters were preserved. It begins with the moving and memorable 'Sullivan Ballou' letter (since made famous by *The Civil War* series), and then asks students to analyze a variety of primary source letters online. Next, students are put into pairs of letter writing correspondents living in 1863. Partners represent a variety of American voices, North and South" (Schur, par. 1, 2). First, students invent an identity. Next, they write letters to one another in character, reacting to events of the Civil War. They are assessed on believability and consistency of characters, reporting of details, authenticity of writing and envelope labeling, conventions, proofreading, etc.

The Schur model can be applied to any time period or theme from epistolary novels, from family letters that the class contributes, or from other print and online letter collections. In each case, students begin by reading and researching a historical letter, collecting clues about context, point of view, and detail. The "Letter Writing Project Ideas" in **Figure 6.4** give a sense of the creativity waiting to be unleashed.

These letter writing activities come with an added bonus—the development of communication skills through letters that also directly support the existing curriculum. Students receive double benefits as they synthesize the content *and* reinforce letter writing skills. One long-time U.S. postal worker reports that he is shocked at how often students from a nearby

Figure 6.4: Letter Writing Project Ideas

Letter Writing Project Ideas

1. Take on the persona of a famous contemporary of the letter writer and respond to the original letter.

2. With a partner, take over the correspondence between the letter writer and the recipient and finish the "story" in a series of letters.

3. Compose a letter from the future that tells the letter writer how the events in the original letter have affected the world today.

4. Send an e-mail to the original writer, updating themes in letters from the past. What is the status of minority groups today? of children? of women workers? of refugees? of soldiers? How have the themes changed over time?

5. Write a short story or a short novel in letter form.

6. Imagine being a soldier in a war or conflict today and write a letter home.

7. E-mail or write a letter to a grandparent comparing life as a teenager today with the grandparent's life as a teenager.

---

university ask him for help in writing and addressing letters correctly. Whether used as an introduction to letter writing or as a review, the final letter project gives students more skill and confidence. As an extension to more traditional letter writing, educators can also use the e-mail ideas in **Figure 6.4** to introduce e-mail etiquette and forms to the next generation of "letter" writers.

Finally, and most importantly, the letter writing conclusion to the letter analysis process meets one of the more challenging *Standards for the English Language Arts* by NCTE and IRA: "Students conduct research on issues and interests by generating ideas and questions, and by posing problems. They gather, evaluate, and synthesize data from a variety of sources (e.g., print and non-print texts, artifacts, people) to communicate their discoveries in ways that suit their purpose and audience." That is the essence of letters.

The Primary Source Librarian in Action

Because of the interdisciplinary nature of letters, the primary source librarian can enhance nearly every curricular area by collecting and marketing authentic letters authored by the famous and the not-so-famous. The checklist below, though not linear, reflects the many ways the primary source librarian can lay the groundwork for learning from letters.

The Primary Source Librarian's Checklist:

❏ Compile a list of epistolary fiction to match the curriculum.
❏ Work with teachers or department chairs to purchase classroom sets of epistolary fiction.
❏ Present ideas at department meetings for incorporating epistolary fiction, using *Letters from Yellowstone* as an example, or...
❏ Lead a staff reading group that focuses on using epistolary novels in teaching, read *Letters from Yellowstone* as a group, and follow through with research about Yellowstone National Park.
❏ Build a collection of Web sites and print materials that feature letters from a variety of historical periods and subjects.
❏ Model an actual letter analysis (**Figures 6.1**, **6.2**, and **6.3**) for teachers and/or students.
❏ Model the research process and online search strategies for students.
❏ Provide teachers with lesson plans for letter and e-mail writing and etiquette or offer to teach it to students. Use **Figure 6.4** for letter writing ideas, and stress content standards.
❏ Offer to participate in student letter writing activities as a correspondent.
❏ Publicize primary source letter projects and recognize collaborating teachers in newsletters and faculty meetings.

Letters, both fictional and actual, personalize and humanize the student's understanding of past events and eras. What begins as the study of another person's eyewitness reports moves through student-driven inquiry and ends with students communicating their new knowledge through the very tool that began this journey—the letter. The library media specialist simply links the letters to the learning.

Chapter

7

Primary Sources
Meet Multimedia

Multimedia and Primary Sources — A Time Warp

Students across the nation are learning new ways to present knowledge through multimedia
applications such as Microsoft's PowerPoint and other slide show presentation software. The
idea of combining historical primary sources with a contemporary presentation tool might
strike some as slightly incongruous, but in fact, it works effectively because of the highly
visual nature of many primary sources. In this chapter, library media specialists will learn
how to structure a complex multimedia unit on the "History of Technology." Students will
select primary sources that illustrate stages of development of a fascinating array of inventions and ideas, enhancing their presentations and deepening their understanding of primary
source evidence. The unit begins and ends with technology, but primary sources drive the
multimedia presentations.

The Dilemma of Technology Responsibility

Today's library media specialist helps create a learning environment without boundaries.
Increasingly, information technologies are moving library services and expertise outside the
library's traditional four walls, extending learners' abilities to conduct inquiry anytime, anywhere. The library media specialist facilitates the inquiry by teaching search strategies and
other information problem solving strategies and by providing quality online resources.
Furthermore, successful multimedia projects depend upon a logical flow from library
research dependent upon technology to the eventual use of technology to communicate that
research. Library media specialists, technology teachers, and classroom teachers collaborate
to assure smooth transitions.

　　　Although the history of technology appears in national and state science standards,
most science programs do not routinely "emphasize abilities associated with the process of

design and fundamental understandings about the enterprise of science and its various linkages with technology" (*National Science Education Standards*). An occasional sidebar in a textbook might point out an invention or an interesting technological development. Rarely can a teacher squeeze a "History of Technology" unit into an already tightly-packed curriculum. Some schools sponsor a yearly "Invention Convention" or a science fair that values creative problem solving through technology. Most school libraries have a few books about inventions and inventors on their shelves.

Even with standards, materials, and a collaborative environment in place, the history of technology crosses over so many curricular borders that no teacher bears obvious responsibility for teaching it. Should it be taught in history classes, science classes, or others? The National Council for the Social Studies declares that "social studies programs should include experiences that provide for the study of relationships among science, technology, and society" (Strand VIII). Carrying the idea of responsibility to a ludicrous level, perhaps music teachers should teach the history of instruments, industrial arts teachers the history of tools, and language arts teachers the history of pen and ink and papermaking. Unfortunately, *shared* responsibility often means *nobody's* responsibility.

Truly, the history of technology can be broad enough or narrow enough to fit nearly every content area, often crossing one line of demarcation into another. In his intriguing book, *Circles: Fifty Round Trips through History, Technology, Science, Culture*, author James Burke laments "the tendency in schools to segment the past into subject areas (history of chemistry, art, music, transportation, and so on) in which advances and discoveries developed the discipline into its modern form…" (15). Just as people in the past were "trapped inside the knowledge context of the time" (14), so are educators trapped inside their content areas. The library media specialist must look for ways to integrate the history of technology whenever and wherever it makes sense, whether in science, social studies, art, an official technology course, or any other subject.

Every school allocates technology staff according to its own values and budget. Some schools employ a "technology teacher," while others hire technicians. Some hold all teachers responsible for teaching technology; still others provide no technology education or support whatsoever. Complicating the picture, the technology teacher often rules the favored kingdom of technology and its prescribed curriculum apart from the library, apart from information literacy, and apart from collaboration and integration. In some cases, the technology teacher has never considered the power of collaboration with colleagues in the library, and yet technology teachers and library media specialists can make superb allies for student learning. The library media specialist must take the first steps toward building this most fruitful of relationships, and the hook might well be the history of technology through multimedia.

Setting the Stage for Inquiry

Working with the technology teacher or any other content area teacher, the library media specialist helps set the stage for inquiry by bringing students and resources together. To introduce the "History of Technology" unit, the teacher/library media specialist team leads students through a brainstorming activity in which they break down broad categories into component inventions or technological breakthroughs. Broad categories include such ideas

Exploring Technology Web Sites

The National Inventors Hall of Fame.
<http://www.invent.org/index.asp>
This online museum celebrates over 150 of the men and women whose patented inventions, life-saving tools, labor-saving devices, and technological innovations have become the basis of the American economy and society.

Greatest Engineering Achievements of the 20th Century.
<http://www.greatachievements.org/greatachievements/indexp.html>
Excellent links to broad categories such as agriculture and food technology, materials technology, clothing and textiles technology, rocket and missile technology, underwater technology, and more.

Events in Science, Mathematics, and Technology.
<http://www.gsu.edu/other/timeline.html>
A comprehensive history with timelines of categorized topics in science, mathematics, and technology.

United States Patent and Trademark Office.
<http://www.uspto.gov/web/offices/ac/ahrpa/opa/kids/index.html>
A great kids' site with streaming video about inventing and patenting, split into K-6, 6-12, and parent and teacher materials.

Jerome and Dorothy Lemelson Center for the Study of Invention and Innovation.
<http://www.si.edu/lemelson/>
A Smithsonian Institution center that encourages inventive creativity in young people and fosters an appreciation for the central role invention and innovation play in the history of the United States.

as weights and measures, timekeeping, printing, power, textiles, photography, medical inventions, sound, flight, radio, or computers. Students choosing to focus on medical inventions might list the stethoscope, anesthetics, hearing aids, syringes, surgical saws, artificial hearts, and prosthetic devices as potential topics.

Another way to structure the investigation is by asking students to explore books or Web sites of inventions, a tactic that values time given to independent inquiry. One book might arrange ideas alphabetically—aspirin, Braille, cereal, dentures, elevators—while another might focus on a particular field of study. Topics are practically limitless.

When given a day to explore the Web and record potential topics, students will almost certainly discover some of the outstanding Web sites annotated in **Figure 7.1**.

Even when tasked with narrowing the list of topic choices, students will discover dozens of quality inventions and technology Web sites during the free-roaming introduction. They should also be encouraged to bookmark potentially helpful Web sites for later use. By the time the students have selected their final topics, they will have built up their own collection of suitable resources.

In anticipation of the multimedia project, the teacher and library media specialist next distribute the list of questions in **Figure 7.2** to guide the inquiry into the history of technology. The questions vary in level of difficulty, and the teacher and library media specialist should consider the ages and abilities of students when selecting them for differentiation. Each question begins with a key word that will later become the title of a slide. The "Source Reminder" after each question requires students to note where they have found their information, and it will help them locate primary sources when they reach that part of the assignment.

As part of a work in progress, the "Research Guide" helps students specifically at the beginning stages of research. The information required is minimal because students are establishing a foundation for more in-depth research. Depending upon the technology selected, some of the questions might be irrelevant or far too difficult, but students should be encouraged to answer as many as possible. By way of example, if a student were to explore the development of the telephone, answers to selected questions 3, 7, and 10 might look like the brief notes below:

3. **PATENT.** Was the technology/invention patented? When? By whom?

   Alexander Graham Bell. 1876. Patent application for an "autograph-telegraph."

   Source Reminder—*<http://jefferson.village.virginia.edu/albell/homepage.html>*
   Gorman— "Alexander Graham Bell's Path to the Telephone."

7. **SOCIAL IMPACT.** Describe the social impact of the technology/invention. What would the world be like without it?

   Cornerstone of modern life. Instant connections between friends, families, businesses, countries. Telephones in films, music lyrics, advertisements, greeting cards. Without the telephone, we would be writing more letters and doing less business.

Research Guide for History of Technology

Technology Topic _____ **Name of Student** _____

1. **INVENTOR/DEVELOPER.** Who invented or developed the technology/invention?

   Source Reminder—

2. **BEFORE THE INVENTION.** What scientific developments preceded the technology/invention?

   Source Reminder—

3. **PATENT.** Was the technology/invention patented? When? By whom?

   Source Reminder—

4. **ADVERTISING.** How was the technology/invention advertised or marketed?

   Source Reminder—

5. **COMPANY**. What company or business was founded to sell the technology/invention?

   Source Reminder—

6. **MUSEUM.** What museum (possibly online) displays the invention?

   Source Reminder—

7. **SOCIAL IMPACT.** Describe the social impact of the technology/ invention. What would the world be like without it?

   Source Reminder—

8. **CHANGE OVER TIME.** How has the technology/invention changed over time?

   Source Reminder—

9. **COLLECTIBLE.** Is anything related to the technology/invention considered "collectible?"

   Source Reminder—

10. **ORGANIZATIONS.** Is there an organization that specializes in the technology/ invention?

    Source Reminder—

11. **FUTURE.** What is the future of the technology/invention?

    Source Reminder—

Source Reminder— *Once Upon a Telephone: An Illustrated Social History*, by Stern and Gwathmey.

10. **ORGANIZATIONS.** Is there an organization that specializes in the technology/invention?

Antique Telephone Collectors Association

Source Reminder— *<http://atcaonline.com/>*

Up to this point, the teaching team has preserved the integrity of the research by intentionally omitting a search for primary sources. When students start looking for photographs, diagrams, letters, and patents, they quickly lose sight of content. Pretty slide shows devoid of content are a common failure in multimedia presentations. Doug Johnson agrees in his "Head for the Edge" column from Linworth Publishing's *The Book Report* magazine, "Pretty pictures and lots of technology will never make up for the lack of interesting ideas and usable information. You can put all the pretty clothes on your dog you want, but he's still a dog" (127).

Connecting Primary Sources to Technology History

Normally a primary source lesson uses the primary source either as an effective means to introduce a lesson or as an analysis complete in itself. The "History of Technology" lesson, on the other hand, begins with extensive exploration and research on a technology topic and ends with a search for primary sources to illustrate each major point. The primary sources provide the visual interest in each multimedia slide. They also reinforce the students' understanding of just how many forms primary sources can take and how important they are to scientific and social history.

Extending the example of the telephone, the library media specialist and cooperating teacher lead the thinking and search process for primary source examples. Given one classroom computer and a projector, a variety of books on inventions (which nearly always give space to the invention of the telephone), and the categories from the **Figure 7.2** "Research Guide," students build a potential list of primary sources to insert into a sample multimedia project on the telephone, as seen below:

INVENTOR— Photograph of Alexander Graham Bell.
BEFORE THE INVENTION— Picture of Samuel F. B. Morse's telegraph; Bell's *Visible Speech Pioneer* publication; early telephone of Johann Philipp Reis; Bell's notebook entry describing his successful experiment with the telephone.
PATENT— Copy of Bell's patent application number 161,739; diagram of Bell's idea (from the *Alexander Graham Bell Family Papers* at the Library of Congress); letters to family members about the patent; competitor Elisha Gray's tardy patent application.
ADVERTISING— Flyer for telephone demonstration at the 1876 Centennial Exhibition in Philadelphia; early catalog advertisements; advertisement for the Princess phone introduced in 1959; cellular phone ads in current newspapers.

COMPANY— Legal papers of Bell Telephone Company, American Bell System, and later AT&T; newspaper articles about the breakup of AT&T in the 1980s; spin-off company pictures of public phone booths, yellow pages, telephone directories.

MUSEUM— Photographs from the Alexander Graham Bell National Historic Site of Canada in Nova Scotia.

SOCIAL IMPACT— Movie posters featuring telephones; photographs of early telephone switchboards; Lily Tomlin as Ernestine; telethons for charity.

CHANGE OVER TIME— Telephone models over the past century; telephone poles and lines; fiber optic cables.

COLLECTIBLE— Antique telephones; glass insulators; telephone memorabilia.

ORGANIZATIONS— Membership forms; show schedules; Web site contact information.

FUTURE— Newspaper articles about telephone trends; cellular phone safety articles; articles about convergence of telephone, video, and related technologies.

As an alternative to the heavily technology-dependent primary source exercise above, the library media specialist can also hand out a timeline of a single technology to encourage creative thinking about primary sources. The library media specialist can easily locate timelines of technology online by adding the word *timeline* to a keyword search. From a simple telephone timeline, students can move from keywords—*women telephone operators*, *underground cables*, *long distance*, *party lines*, *direct dial*, *dial telephones*, *area codes*, *cordless telephones*, *optical fiber*, *caller id*—to primary source examples. Timelines particularly resonate with science teachers because of their focus on scientific breakthroughs. A timeline approach also forces students to search for primary sources related to each point on the timeline rather than merely scanning pages from a Dorling Kindersley publication!

At this stage, students have completed their surface exploration of a technology topic and brainstormed primary source options. Now they need time to investigate their own topics in more depth and to discover primary sources to match their questions. Multimedia frenzy soon dominates the classroom scene.

Multimedia—A Craze or Just Plain Crazy?

After the initial excitement over multimedia in the classroom, many educators have stepped back to take a more discriminating look at the benefits to learning. Far too often, the bells and whistles of multimedia overpower actual learning, but the library media specialist can head off disaster by communicating with teachers about some of the lessons learned from multimedia projects gone sour.

Throughout the steps of research and identification of primary sources, the library media specialist provides a storyboard template that helps students plan and organize their presentations. Many library media specialists use the "Storyboard for Hypermedia Project" developed by Joyce Valenza for her 1998 ALA *Power Tools* packet of essential forms and presentations—a must-buy for every school library. The storyboard in **Figure 7.3** owes its origins to Valenza's model, but it has been customized to fit both the PowerPoint software and the "History of Technology" project.

Figure 7.3: PowerPoint Storyboard

Name of Student

Layout Design

Source:

Author _____

Title of Work/Web page _____

Title of Article _____

Name of Publisher _____

Place of Publication _____

Date of Publication _____

Date Accessed _____

URL or Database _____

PowerPoint Storyboard

Technology Name _____

Slide Title _____

Slide Number 1 2 3 4 5 6 7 8 9 10

Text. Write text points next to the bullets below.

_____

• _____

• _____

• _____

• _____

Description and URL of Primary Source Graphic

_____

_____

Animations or sounds to reinforce points

_____

_____

Students fill out one storyboard per slide, perhaps an overuse of paper but ultimately a practical solution to the sorry state of most multimedia presentations. The teacher must decide how many slides to require, a decision based on student feedback about their success or failure finding answers to the worksheet questions. Students should always be allowed to substitute slides more meaningful to their topics, using slides such as "Interesting Trivia," "The Competition," or "How It Works."

The library media specialist should share the wisdom that comes from witnessing repeated multimedia assignments with every first-time multimedia teacher. Accumulated PowerPoint "wisdom" can be communicated by the library media specialist through newsletters, informal conversations, and handouts such as the one in **Figure 7.4**, "PowerPoint Pointers from Teachers and Librarians Who Learned the Hard Way."

Copyright Conundrums

Carol Simpson declares in her Linworth publication, *Copyright for Schools: A Practical Guide, 3rd edition*, that multimedia is "a copyright infringement nightmare" (67)! A single multimedia presentation might include music, video, still images, and graphics, all with different copyrights. For example, if students were to use a sound recording of "The Telephone Hour" from the 1960 musical *Bye Bye Birdie* as a primary source for the social impact of the telephone, they would have to deal with copyrights of the songwriter, the lyricist, the producer, the Broadway singers, the instrumentalists, the recording studio, and more. If they inserted a photograph of the original production number, still more copyright holders would complicate the situation. Suddenly the question of whether Hugo and Kim got pinned hardly seems worth the bother, even if they are "goin' steady for good."

Fortunately, students in non-profit schools have some "fair use" breathing room. "The new agreement on Fair Use Guidelines for Educational Multimedia provides concrete limits on the types and amounts of material that may be included in works created by teachers and students" (Simpson 68). It is essential for all library media specialists to read the guidelines, understand the limits, and teach students and colleagues the ethics of copyright. First, this means following rules of retention, access, and quantity. Second, it means requiring bibliographic citations. The source lines on each PowerPoint storyboard prompt students to gather the necessary items for citing their research and primary sources.

Teachers should always assign a "Works Cited" slide at the end of a multimedia presentation. The multimedia guidelines require it. Carol Simpson adds another expectation: "The opening screen of the multimedia work and any accompanying printed materials must contain a notice that the work contains copyrighted materials under the fair use exemption of U.S. Copyright Law" (70).

Multimedia units give students frequent opportunities to practice social responsibility. As students learn to credit sources and acknowledge copyright law, they look to the guidance of responsible library media specialists and teachers who model the policies that protect intellectual property.

Figure 7.4: PowerPoint Pointers

PowerPoint Pointers from Teachers and Librarians Who Learned the Hard Way

1. Spend 15 minutes the first day showing students how and where to save work. Spend 10 minutes the second day showing them how to find their saved work. Spend 10 minutes at the end of the second day showing them AGAIN how to save. Reinforce the saving day after day after day after day.

2. Spend the entire first day on basics. Teach your students how to open the program, how to create one new slide, how to choose the slide format, how to insert text, how to create one more new slide rather than a whole new presentation, how to save, how to find and open the file, and how to close the file and quit the program.

3. For teaching purposes, have all the students create the same first practice slide. Some teachers like to have their students create an "ugly slide" in order to teach good (and bad) design. Students can delete their ugly slides before beginning work on the actual assignment.

4. Do NOT teach any PowerPoint before you yourself have gone through a personal tutorial with technology or library staff. We will cover how to save, where to save, how to find lost files, and how best to manage the PowerPoint classroom. You will be ever so grateful at the end of the project.

5. Set an absolute, non-negotiable due date. No excuses! No begging! If you don't stick to your guns, you will go crazy and so will we, and you will never want to teach PowerPoint again. Don't be nice about this one.

6. Don't let students work on their projects at home even if you are a nice person. We always have problems with compatibility of program versions, saving to disk, corrupted files, etc. Take it from us, these problems are not worth the time it takes to fix them.

7. Require that students do their writing before actually beginning their PowerPoint projects. Correct for grammar and spelling.

8. Require students to plan their slide shows and lay them out on a storyboard or a graphic organizer. The library media center provides customized graphic organizers for PowerPoint presentations.

9. Put all content into slides before doing any fun stuff. Graphics, animation, and sound should come last.

10. If students need extra time, they may sign up for after-school help. Do not, we repeat, DO NOT EVEN THINK ABOUT being flexible with the due date unless you want them to pluck you (and us) like a dead chicken.

11. Tell your students that you will be available for after-school help on their projects, but only if they sign up with you in advance.

12. Ask students to insert scanned images or graphics from the Internet directly into PowerPoint or save them to a folder on the network server under the teacher's name. The network should eliminate the need to print.

13. Set a maximum number of slides. Students don't know when to quit.

14. Grade on content more than glitz.

Assessing Multimedia Projects

Numerous educators have developed excellent multimedia assessment rubrics and posted them online. The popular *Kathy Schrock's Guide for Educators*, sponsored by Discovery School.com, offers a comprehensive list of Web links to assessment tools. Joan M. Vandervelde's outstanding PowerPoint rubric includes assessments for research and note taking, pre-plan/storyboard, introduction, content, text elements, layout, citations, graphics, sound, animation, writing mechanics, and teamwork. The library media specialist and collaborating teacher can design their own rubrics to reflect the assigned topics and to emphasize the primary source nature of the multimedia assignment, but they can certainly learn from these outstanding examples.

The Primary Source Librarian in Action

Only the imaginations of the library media specialist, the collaborating teacher, and the students can limit the multimedia and primary source connections in a history of technology unit. While a high school physics teacher might ask students to illustrate a timeline of atomic power, an elementary science teacher might ask younger students to find primary sources for a history of recycling. For a unit on advertising, students in a social studies class search for company histories and pictures of children playing with popular toys, such as the slinky, the erector set, silly putty, roller skates, the yo-yo, tinkertoys, and more. No matter what the subject, primary sources enrich and personalize the study, and they help students recognize that they are surrounded by the primary source evidence of countless scientific and technological developments.

The primary source librarian supports multimedia presentations both as a technology expert and as an expert in locating primary sources. As usual, the best units begin with collaboration, and the library media specialist keeps tabs at every stage.

The Primary Source Librarian's Checklist:

☐ Build collaborative relationships with science and technology teachers as well as with any colleague willing to try a new combination—primary sources and multimedia.

☐ Especially encourage the technology teacher to try a "History of Technology" collaboration that combines library research with multimedia lessons.

☐ Provide lists of potential topics along with technology or invention Web sites for early exploration of topics, as in **Figure 7.1**.

☐ With the collaborating teacher, develop lists of questions that guide inquiry and define eventual multimedia slides, or use the **Figure 7.2** "Research Guide."

☐ Model research on the telephone or another topic of choice by demonstrating searches for primary sources for several categories in the **Figure 7.2** "Research Guide."

☐ As an alternative, provide a timeline of technology, and match timeline elements with primary source examples.

☐ Customize a multimedia storyboard for the teacher and class to use in planning and organizing the presentation, using the **Figure 7.3** "PowerPoint Storyboard" as a guide.

- Share pointers with collaborating teachers on classroom organization and technology skills needed for a successful multimedia project, using **Figure 7.4**, "PowerPoint Pointers from Teachers and Librarians Who Learned the Hard Way."
- Discuss and model copyright compliance, and help students develop citation skills.
- Collaborate with the teacher to develop an assessment rubric that includes primary source goals, content expectations, and technical multimedia skills.
- Attend final student presentations. Invite administrators, parents, and other supporters.
- Always acknowledge the accomplishments of students and collaborating teachers through newsletters, faculty meetings, and other public forums.

Most people fail to consider the educational value of primary sources beyond the history curriculum, but every scientific and technological development leaves its own fascinating trail of evidence. Through letters, photographs, and diagrams left by scientists and inventors, students glimpse creative minds in action. Through film, advertisements, and newspaper articles, they form a picture of how innovation and invention inform their world. In the "History of Technology" unit, the products of the past meet the technologies of today, and the primary source librarian forges the connection.

Chapter

8

From Biography to Artifacts

Biography Beginnings — Primary Source Endings

Normally when students attempt to interpret the forces of history and ideas based on the evidence of primary sources, they *start* with the primary sources as a foundation for learning. Reversing the process, this chapter considers the possibility of *beginning* with the study of people — the exceedingly common and comfortable biography assignment — and ending with imaginative, student-produced primary source facsimiles. Because biography lessons pose little risk to teachers who might mistrust new, untested primary source curriculum, the library media specialist can sometimes use biography as a gateway to incorporating primary sources.

A Standards-Based Rationale for Biography

Biography offers exceptional flexibility for the classroom. Teachers can opt to allow students to select their biography subjects according to personal interests, but wise teachers meet specific curricular standards through biography, limiting assignment parameters by ethnicity, gender, historical time period, nationality, profession, or other groupings that match content standards. Beginning as early as the primary grades, the *National Standards for History* require students to "describe how historical figures in the United States and other parts of the world have advanced the rights of individuals and promoted the common good, and identify character traits such as persistence, problem solving, moral responsibility, and respect for others that made them successful" (Standard 4C). This single history/biography standard might encompass as broad a selection of topics as the civil rights movement, influential Native Americans, child labor activists, the founders of the nation, women's history, famous immigrants, people who have overcome disabilities, and heroes.

Other standards in a wide range of content areas—science, art, ancient history, literature, and more—call for biographical studies as well. For example, the *National Science Education Standards* fold in biography lessons under the history of science and science as a human endeavor categories: "Many individuals have contributed to the traditions of science. Studying some of these individuals provides further understanding of scientific inquiry, science as a human endeavor, the nature of science, and the relationships between science and society" (Content Standard G, Grades 5–8, par. 7).

In short, biography standards exist for all age levels and all content areas, and biography units therefore rank consistently high among teacher requests for collection and library research support. Every library media specialist has scrambled to fill the requests of students who suddenly appear with an assignment to find a biography—*any* biography—without prior teacher/library media specialist consultation. Every library media specialist can relate to the colleague who said, "I quit buying sports biographies the year I bought four Bo Jackson books and he blew out his knee. The next year, nobody knew who he was!"

A proactive library media specialist anticipates biography units and seeks out teachers to collaborate on curriculum. The team develops standards-based biography units dependent upon library collections, both print and online, that are pre-identified and appropriate. More and more, online sources have become the collection fillers for the inevitable surprise requests, so it is essential that the library media specialist collect a ready list of quality bookmarked biography Web sites, beginning with a "megasite" such as "Lives, the Biography Resource" (http://www.amillionlives.com/). This award-winning site links to thousands of biographies and groups of biographies "about people who share a common profession, historical era or geography," and it offers bonus links to numerous primary sources that include memoirs, diaries, letters, and more.

Biography—Who Writes It? How Do They Write It? Why Do They Write It?

The integration of primary sources into biography studies also encourages students to think about how biographies are written and why. To reinforce student comprehension of the place of primary sources in historical research, the library media specialist and teacher partners can facilitate a class discussion about the biographer's craft. The "Biography Discussion Questions" in **Figure 8.1** will help students think critically about biography as an interpretation of primary sources, even sometimes a controversial one. Students can also discuss the questions in small groups and "report out" during a wrap-up session.

The discussion should help students understand that biography is much more than the factual chronicling of a life. Rather than trust every biographer to report "the truth," students need to become more discriminating readers of biography. They need to develop a sort of consumer's guide approach to biography research, thinking critically about sources, integrity, solid reporting, biases, and thoughtful inquiry on the part of each biographer. They need to be able to distinguish manipulation from skilled research, and sensationalism from honest interpretation.

Students might be surprised to learn that "good biographers go the extra mile to check out everything, never settling for secondary data when additional effort might uncover primary data….The best biographers never use secondary sources until all leads for primary sources are exhausted" (Weinberg, 30). *Smithsonian* magazine editor Carey Winfrey reports

Figure 8.1: Biography Discussion Questions

> **Biography Discussion Questions**
>
> 1. Who writes biographies? Journalists? College professors? Family members?
> 2. What (or who) gives biographers the authority to write on particular subjects?
> 3. Do biographers just report the facts of a person's life, or do they interpret them?
> 4. How or where do biographers find the primary sources upon which to base a biography?
> 5. Do biographers copy from one another?
> 6. How do skilled biographers fill in the gaps about a person's life?
> 7. How do historians differ from biographers? Do they respect each other?
> 8. Why do so many people read biographies?
> 9. Why do biographers continue to write about people who already have dozens of biographies written about them?
> 10. Do living subjects of biographies have a right to privacy?
> 11. What are the qualities of a good biography?
> 12. Is VH1's "Behind the Music" program "good" biography?
> 13. What is the best way for a student to learn about a famous person?
> 14. What biography sources can students trust?

respected biographer Landon Y. Jones's slightly earthier assessment: "A requisite for writing this kind of book ... is 'a cast-iron butt, since you spend a lot of time sitting in libraries leafing through archival collections'" (9).

Apart from being one of the most popular and lucrative "genres" in publishing, biography differs significantly from strict historical writing in its power to personalize history. Biographer and essayist Michael Holroyd values the way "biography can humanize our history" (21). He compares biography to the tradition of storytelling: "By recreating the past we are calling on the same magic as our forebears did with stories of their ancestors round the fires under the night skies. The need to do this, to keep death in its place, lies deep in human nature, and the art of biography arises from that need" (30).

Teaching Students to Evaluate Biography Sources

As an information literacy follow-up to the previous discussion, students can become even more discriminating consumers of biographies by comparing actual biographical sources. To begin this exercise, the teacher divides the class into groups, and the library media specialist furnishes each group with the following biography sources on a single historical character:

1. A full-length biography in book form.
2. A collective biography that includes the person.
3. A collective biography reference book, such as the *Dictionary of American Biography*.

4. A printed copy of a biography from an online subscription database (GALE, EBSCO, BigChalk, etc.).
5. A printed copy of a biography from a general Web site.
6. A copy of an article from a magazine such as *Biography* or *People Weekly*.

Obviously, the quality of sources may vary across groups, but the point of the exercise is to help students think critically about a realistic range of sources, not to find the perfect source. Students select three of the sources and examine each one separately, looking for evidence of the biographer's credentials, coverage, balance or bias, and presentation or design. Next, they compare them with each other as they answer the four categories of questions in the **Figure 8.2** "Biography Source Evaluation."

In this activity, students in groups must reach consensus as they rate each feature with +, –, or ?. This activity is designed to generate discussions about the pros and cons of assorted published biographies. Students will argue for positive or negative ratings, particularly in the "balance" category. They must decide if advertising distracts from the biography, for instance, or if a strong ideological stance indicates a negative bias. Younger students will need more directed discussion, but they can still use this exercise to increase critical evaluation skills.

In the past several years, Web site evaluation instruments have proliferated on educational sites on the Internet, and the majority of criteria in these tools work equally well for evaluating print resources. To locate dozens of instruments for use with classes, the library media specialist can enter the phrase "*web page evaluation*" or any number of variations on the concept into any search engine. *Kathy Schrock's Guide for Educators* links to numerous evaluation tools (http://school.discovery.com/schrockguide/eval.html). If the collaborating teacher prefers to concentrate on Web evaluations alone, the library media specialist might also develop comparison charts for biography entries from a subscription database, an online encyclopedia, and a general biography Web site ("A & E Biography," for instance). No matter how the details change to reflect the evaluation goals, the library media specialist stands always at the service of the cooperating teacher to support student learning through technology and information literacy tools.

Beyond Basic Biography

Chapter 4, "Primary Source Analysis Techniques," focused heavily on the importance of developing questions that pull essential meanings from primary sources. Whether using primary or secondary sources, students developing information literacy skills always return to the importance of questions, questions, questions. Jamie McKenzie, one of the foremost advocates for purposeful and sensible integration of educational technologies in support of learning, has coined the essence of this concept in a byline for his monthly publication, *From Now On — The Educational Technology Journal*: "The question is the answer." He believes that the quality of student learning always rests on the quality of questions, an observation that certainly holds true for the study of biography. As he states on his outstanding "Biography Maker" Web page:

Figure 8.2: Biography Source Evaluation

BIOGRAPHY SOURCE EVALUATION	SOURCE #1	SOURCE #2	SOURCE #3
Name of Biography Subject:			
Biographer:			
Does the source establish the authority, professional training, or credentials of a particular biographer or editorial group?			
Is there any additional indication of the sources (including primary sources) or the research behind the information?			
Coverage:			
Does the source give too little or too much information?			
Does the source cover the entire life of the subject of the biography?			
Does the source situate the subject within its historical context?			
Does the source offer options for further study (bibliography, links, etc.)?			
Is the information current?			
Balance:			
Does the content show a bias or slant?			
Does the source include advertising?			
Does the author/publisher represent a particular group, either political or ideological?			
Are statistics credited?			
Is there evidence of a balance of primary sources to support the content?			
Presentation:			
Is the source clearly and logically organized?			
Is the source without errors in spelling, punctuation, or grammar?			
Is the source appropriate for the age and ability level of the students?			
Is the source easy to use?			
Is the source visually appealing?			

A great biography is driven by great questions.
Boring questions produce boring answers.
Boring answers put readers to sleep.
Simple lists of facts are a bit like dry cereal …
no milk … no fruit … no taste!

Most educators have read too many "dry cereal" biography reports, sadly unaware that they have the power to change the biography experience from one of uninspired regurgitation of birth dates, death dates, and chronological listings of life facts simply by asking better questions. In their defense, many teachers of elementary and middle school students do inject enthusiasm into biography assignments by requiring their students to "dress up as the person" for an oral presentation. In spite of this single creative element, however, they often accept the same boring written report as evidence of research.

Jamie McKenzie has developed the following list of probing questions for biographies to help students explore the human drama that they so often miss:

- In what ways was the life remarkable?
- In what ways was the life despicable?
- In what ways was the life admirable?
- What human qualities were most influential in shaping the way this person lived and influenced his or her times?
- Which quality or trait proved most troubling and difficult?
- Which quality or trait was most beneficial?
- Did this person make any major mistakes or bad decisions? If so, what were they and how would you have chosen and acted differently if you were in their shoes?
- What are the two or three most important lessons you or any other young person might learn from the way this person lived?
- Some people say you can judge the quality of a person's life by the enemies they make. Do you think this is true of your person's life? Explain why or why not.
- An older person or mentor is often very important in shaping the lives of gifted people by providing guidance and encouragement. To what extent was this true of your person? Explain.
- Many people act out of a "code" or a set of beliefs which dictate choices. It may be religion or politics or a personal philosophy. To what extent did your person act by a code or act independently of any set of beliefs? Were there times when the code was challenged and impossible to follow?
- What do you think it means to be a hero? Was your person a "hero?" Why? Why not? How is a hero different from a celebrity?[1]

Once students begin to look for answers to the questions above, they will read with a deeper purpose, looking beyond mere facts to uncover the real personalities, quirks, foibles, talents, and contradictions of their subjects. They will begin to recognize that skilled

[1] Jamie McKenzie. Used with permission.

biographers invite readers to explore beneath surface dates and events to discover the core causes of behaviors and to piece together the human puzzles of the past.

"Biography in a Box"—First Steps

Up to this point, students have discussed biography as a genre and evaluated sources in a rather cerebral preparation for their research on a specific person. They have established the link between strong questions and worthwhile research. As they begin gathering information, they will need to shift their thinking to a highly visual, hands-on presentation format appropriate for all age levels—"Biography in a Box"—in which they will decorate the outside of a box, fill it with the written evidence of their research, and insert an appropriate self-created artifact. All three elements—an artistic interpretation of the life studied, a solid written component, and an artifact that reflects the essence of each subject—require students to apply rather than simply regurgitate their research.

In this project, students bring to class cereal boxes (or shoe boxes, detergent boxes … any boxes large enough to hold an eventual "artifact") labeled with their names. They will also need art supplies such as markers, paints, decorative papers, scissors, glue, glitter, and other hobby store miscellany. As they research, they may wish to photocopy or print out drawings or photographs of their subjects and their "works." Throughout the project, they need to be mindful of ways to interpret visually the life of their subject.

After students have completed reading and taking notes on the assigned or self-selected biography subject, they cover the outside of the box with materials that reflect their subject's time period and/or accomplishments. They might identify the box with their subject's name in bold letters along with a photograph. In many cases they will embellish the box with original art work, documents, quotations, drawings, and other two-dimensional items that begin to illustrate their subject's life story. In other words, they will copy primary sources to decorate the outsides of their box "reports."

One student might drape Elizabeth Cady Stanton's box with a "Votes for Women" sash. Another might make a small pastel reproduction of *Mother and Child* from the Art Institute of Chicago to decorate painter Mary Cassatt's box. Other boxes take on the colors of a nation's flag, the portrait of a president, the pressed flowers of a botanist, or the bars of a dissident's cell. By deciding how to reflect and interpret a person's life through the decorations, students prepare themselves for the final representation of their biography—the three-dimensional artifact that they will place inside the box.

Before students place the final artifact inside the box, however, they must return to their basic biographical research in order to fill out a packet of five 4" × 6" research cards on card stock provided by the teacher. These cards, to be placed together in the box, replace the traditional biography *report*, although the first "Biographical Information" card does require, well, a bit of "dry cereal" information to demonstrate the student's basic historical knowledge (**Figure 8.3**).

On the second, third, and fourth cards (**Figure 8.4**) students write short, original paragraphs based either on selected questions from McKenzie's list or their own carefully-developed inquiries. On the "Action Card," a student might discuss why the Oglala Sioux war leader Crazy Horse remarked that it was "a good day to die" as he led the attack on Custer's troops at Little Big Horn (*DISCovering Multicultural America*, par. 16). On the

"Character Card," a student might look at how Crazy Horse's patriotism and love of his people made him view the white man's diplomacy as skilled deception. The "Influence Card" might discuss Crazy Horse's victory at Little Big Horn as symbolically important but essentially hollow. Finally, on the fifth card, students complete a full list of bibliographic citations for the sources used during their research.

When a teacher moves biography studies toward the inquiry approach of this assignment, the students may express dismay, for it rises far above the low-level reporting that they have experienced through years of comfortable yet uninspiring biography assignments. The deceptively simple "action," "character," and "influence" cards actually require high-level thinking and analysis for students to synthesize their learning into succinct paragraph form. Furthermore, the quality of the results depends on the quality of the questions, a principle at the heart of information literacy.

"Biography In A Box"—Creating Original Artifacts

For the final task, students create an original artifact that *might* have belonged to the subject of their biography. As students read about the life of a famous person, they begin to imagine what their characters might have carried with them, what they might have displayed in their houses, or what they might have valued enough to pass on to their own children. Using historical figures as examples, students can brainstorm artifact ideas. What were the products

Figure 8.3: Biographical Information Card

Biographical Information Card

FRONT   #1

Name:

Date of Birth:

Date of Death:

Known for:

BACK

Basic biographical information:

-
-
-
-
-
-
-
-
-
-

Student name:

Date:

Figure 8.4: Biography Cards

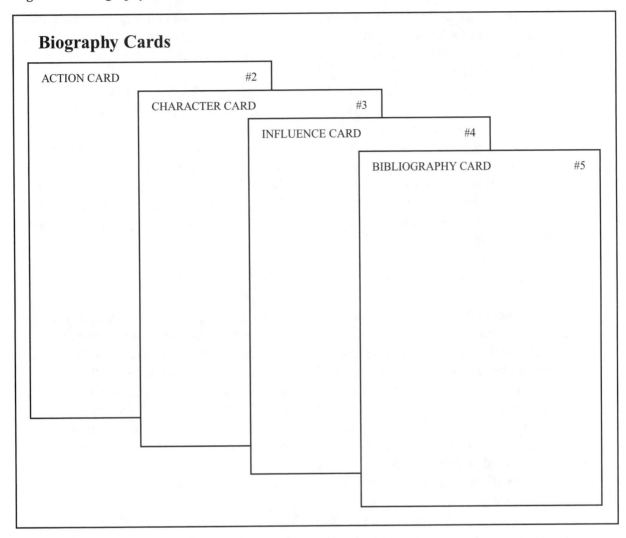

of Benjamin Franklin's work in applied science and invention? What kinds of specimens did Charles Darwin collect as the H. M. S. Beagle followed the coasts of South America? What did pioneer men and women carry in covered wagons? What "artifact" caused the tragic death of dancer Isadora Duncan? What artifacts, in effect, give meaning to the study of a person's life?

In her most recent book, *The Middle of Everywhere: The World's Refugees Come to Our Town*, psychologist Mary Pipher examines the experiences of dozens of refugees who have emigrated within the last decade to the Midwest city of Lincoln, Nebraska. In a touching chapter about refugee children, she notes the horrible past traumas suffered by many of the children and the huge acculturation hurdles they still face. Many have arrived in the United States with nothing but a few precious family artifacts. When the author visits an English Language Learner class, she discovers, "Almost all these kids carried totems of their former countries. Mai had her mother's picture. Ignazio wore a leather belt made by his uncle, and Pavel still had his favorite toys from Russia. Fatima carried a twig with one green leaf that her grandmother sent her from Iraq. Walat spoke of the Turkish delight that his family saved for special days. Deena's grandmother sent her spinach gum that she passed around" (147).

These "totems" reflect the essence of this special group of children. Each tells a story, and each represents the nature and memories of a cherished former identity. Similarly, the students' final "Biography in a Box" task is to imagine and create an artifact that best reflects the essence of their subject.

The student-designed artifact helps solidify the concept of primary sources when the student becomes responsible for explaining its relationship to the subject of each biography. In one actual classroom incident, a student gleefully reported that she had already decided which artifact to place in her Susan B. Anthony box—a Susan B. Anthony dollar! Her classmates protested that there was no way the nineteenth-century suffragist would have carried a coin minted late in the twentieth century (1979). An artifact must be contemporaneous to the person studied, or "That's cheating," they pointed out. The student's peers communicated the concept of primary sources far more effectively than any teacher could have dreamed of doing.

Using Biography to Teach Themes

When an entire class explores one theme through the "Biography in a Box" lesson, the students build shared knowledge that strengthens discussions throughout the unit and the school year. In anticipation of biography collaborations, the library media specialist can start collecting resources immediately for the multicultural and historical themes outlined below.

Teachers and librarians can introduce students to an effective "Biography in a Box" lesson early in the school year as part of Hispanic Heritage Month from September 15 to October 15. Emphasizing the importance of "Latino Legacies," Lawrence M. Small writes, "Because the founding heritage of vast regions of this country was Hispanic, no account of the past—and no understanding of the present—can be complete if it does not acknowledge that indelible cultural imprint, which is vivid still and will become even more pronounced in the decades ahead" (14).

Conducting a simple Web search on *hispanic heritage month*, the library media specialist brings up dozens of lessons and activities to support teachers. For example, free Web resources for "Celebrating Hispanic Heritage" from Gale Group's commercial subscription site (http://www.galegroup.com/free_resources/chh/index.htm) include biographies of significant Hispanic people that range from novelist Isabel Allende to baseball slugger Sammy Sosa. Students can "take a Hispanic culture quiz, follow a timeline of events that helped shape the Hispanic culture, explore Hispanic holidays and musical genres…, or visit other pertinent sites and find suggestions for further readings" (par. 2). Via other links, the library media specialist can discover U. S. Census Bureau statistics for Hispanic Heritage Month (http://www.census.gov/Press-Release/fs97-10.html), order attractive posters, or lead teachers to extensive support materials from the Public Broadcasting System, Education World, and other dependable educational sites.

Moving to November, "Biography in a Box" meets National American Indian Heritage Month. In a proclamation in 2002, President George W. Bush declared, "During American Indian Heritage Month, we celebrate the rich cultural traditions and proud ancestry of American Indians and Alaska Natives, and we recognize the vital contributions these groups have made to the strength and diversity of our society." (par. 1). Native American studies match the social studies curriculum at specific grade levels, and November is the perfect time to plan a thematic biography unit for those grades. The library media specialist can find excellent teaching resources at the Smithsonian's National Museum of the American Indian (http://www.nmai.si.edu/index.asp) as well as hundreds of Native American biography Web sites.

February's Black History Month highlights the rich and diverse history of African Americans. Nationally celebrated since 1976, its roots reach back over seventy-five years to the early advocacy of African American historian and teacher Carter G. Woodson. While an unfocused Google search on "black history month" displays an overwhelming 1,120,000 hits, the Association for the Study of African American Life and History offers a learning resource page of "Black History Month and Kit Themes" (http://www.asalh.com/blackhistorytheme.htm) that lists national themes through 2010. The U. S. Department of State's "African American History Month" page starts with a history of the celebration (http://usinfo.state.gov/usa/blackhis/history.htm) and provides a gateway to carefully chosen links to Black History Month sites through the U. S. Census Bureau's "Profile America" series, the Librarians' Index to the Internet, The History Channel, and other reliable sites. Students will gain essential perspectives on African American contributions as they search for biographies from link to link.

Following closely on the heels of February's Black History Month comes National Women's History Month in March. The National Women's History Project (http://www.nwhp.org/), founded in 1980, is an educational nonprofit organization whose mission "is to recognize and celebrate the diverse and historic accomplishments of women by providing information and educational materials and programs" (par. 1). Its Web site offers program ideas for community organizations, teachers, librarians, workplaces, parents, and students. Just as Black History Month concentrates on annual themes, the National Women's History Project features yearly groups of women's biographies by theme. For example, in 2002, the project honored Alice Coachman, Dorothy Height, Dolores Huerta, Gerda Lerner, Patsy T. Mink, and Mary Louise Defender Wilson to illustrate its theme of "Women Sustaining the American Spirit." A "Biography Center" links to stories of past honorees. For a special event, the library media specialist can use the Web site to locate performers by state, arranging a school visit by actors portraying Amelia Earhart, Mary Todd Lincoln, and many others.

"Biography in a Box" strengthens all major multicultural celebrations, but librarians and teachers hardly need limit biography lessons to four areas alone. A serious look at the curriculum will uncover biography connections to immigration, westward movement, explorers, civil rights, wars, scientists, mathematicians, writers, world leaders, heroes, inventors, artists, musicians, children, athletes, citizens of every state … a rich and varied pool of fascinating lives and contributions. Students will discover multiple ways to celebrate famous lives through their own handmade artifacts.

The Primary Source Librarian in Action

Through the lessons in this chapter, students solidify the concept of primary sources and artifacts as an essential foundation of biography studies. The biography-artifact connection helps students meet *National Standards for History* that include "describing the past on its own terms, through the eyes and experiences of those who were there, as revealed through their literature, diaries, letters, debates, arts, artifacts, and the like" (Historical Thinking Standard 2A).

The Primary Source Librarian's Checklist:

- ☐ Collect biography standards in all content areas.
- ☐ Collect biography resources by ethnicity, gender, historical time period, nationality, profession — whatever fits the curriculum.
- ☐ Pre-identify and bookmark excellent biography Web sites, using them to supplement print collections.
- ☐ Anticipate biography units and seek out teachers to collaborate on curriculum that guarantees standards-based biography units.
- ☐ Provide **Figure 8.1** "Biography Discussion Questions" to teachers, and offer to lead discussions of the biographer's craft.
- ☐ Introduce the **Figure 8.2** "Biography Source Evaluation" and select multiple biography sources for the activity.
- ☐ Discuss "dry cereal" biography reports and strong questioning techniques from Jamie McKenzie's "Biography Maker."
- ☐ Co-develop the "Biography in a Box" assignment based on the theme or group of biographies selected by the cooperating teacher.
- ☐ Provide "Biographical Information" cards (**Figures 8.3** and **8.4**).
- ☐ During scheduled research, help students identify primary sources related to their subjects and discuss ways of producing three-dimensional artifacts.
- ☐ Display finished projects in the library media center.
- ☐ Use student work to interest other teachers in enhancing biography studies through primary sources.

By the time students have completed the activities of this chapter, they will better understand what biographer Gale E. Christianson meant when he wrote about researching contemporary figures: "…primary sources comprise more than words and images captured on paper; they are the roof under which one's subject was born, the schoolhouse where he learned his ABCs, the neighborhood streets where he walked hand in hand with his high school sweetheart, and, if one is very lucky, the living memories of those who grew up with him and took his measure, as the cliché goes, 'way back when'" (73). Students will hardly fit a hometown into a box, but they will certainly find themselves contemplating the artifacts that surround and define a life.

Chapter

9

The Art of Geography

Art As a Primary Source

Educators seldom categorize works of art as primary sources, but to ignore art as a primary source would be to miss an exciting and unusual path to knowledge. If an artist personally witnesses a scene or an event and then produces a work of art that interprets it, the product does indeed qualify as "firsthand evidence of historical events or periods." In fact, original works of art share a number of characteristics with other types of primary sources, as seen in **Figure 9.1**, "Art As Primary Source."

When combined with "academic" subjects, the visual arts help students understand "how images are used to communicate important ideas, thoughts, and feelings in our daily lives and those recorded throughout civilization" (*National Standards for Arts Education*). Fortunately, librarians, teachers, and students need not be experts in art criticism to use fine art effectively as a primary source. Armed with basic definitions of the elements and principles of art, students can explore and interpret works of art, make connections to a variety of disciplines, and apply the critical thinking of an art historian to the understanding of other concepts and times.

This chapter specifically describes a unit that builds comprehension of the five themes of geography through the study of American landscape painting. Following the three-step process below, the library media specialist, in collaboration with the classroom teacher, facilitates learning about the two subjects separately before integrating them in a final analysis activity. The teaching team:

1. Leads students through a concept mapping exercise to break down the elements of each geographic theme.
2. Models how to search for and "read" a painting that illustrates a geographic theme.
3. Helps students select and analyze paintings, connect them to the geographic themes, and justify their choices through a three-paragraph writing activity.

Figure 9.1: Art as Primary Source

Art As Primary Source		
Characteristics of Primary Sources	Work of Art	Other Primary Sources
They represent the viewpoint of one eyewitness.	✓	✓
The creator interprets reality, deciding what is important or true.	✓	✓
They reflect the times. What is beautiful? What is valued? What are the prevailing attitudes?	✓	✓
They are created for a particular audience.	✓	✓
They are created for a specific reason.	✓	✓
One can make both objective and subjective observations about them.	✓	✓
One can ask what is excluded as well as what is included.	✓	✓

Mapping the Themes of Geography

In 1984, a joint committee of the National Council for Geographic Education and the Association of American Geographers published *Guidelines for Geographic Education, Elementary and Secondary Schools*. Social studies teachers quickly embraced the guidelines, which were organized around the "Five Themes of Geography." The five interrelated themes—location, place, human-environment interaction, movement, and region—gave geography educators a framework for teaching an extremely complex and constantly changing subject.

Over the years, educators have developed hundreds of activities to teach the five themes. At the National Geographic Society Web site, for example, one can find clever teaching ideas such as asking students to imagine how their school would change if someone were to pick it up like a toy block and set it down in a totally different location (http://www.nationalgeographic.com/resources/ngo/education/themes.html). On the Education World Web site, the twenty-five lessons in "Five Times Five: Five Activities for Teaching Geography's Five Themes" describe several hands-on, arts-based geography activities (http://www.education-world.com/a_lesson/lesson071.shtml). These lessons and others should become part of a continuous collaborative focus with the proactive library media specialist building a collection of Web sites of "five themes" lesson plans to file away with other bookmarked teaching aids.

Unfortunately, "Five Themes" teaching materials rarely give clear or concise definitions of the five themes. Instead, they generally begin with lengthy, confusing explanations followed by lists of examples under each theme. The National Geographic Web pages mentioned above, for instance, vaguely explain the third theme in the following way: "The environment means different things to different people, depending on their cultural backgrounds and technological resources. In studying human/environment interaction, geographers look at all the effects…" (3). Likewise, the "movement" theme begins more as a series of examples than as a strict definition: "People interact with other people, places, and things almost every day of their lives. They travel from one place to another; they communicate with each other; and they rely upon products, information, and ideas that come from beyond their immediate environment" (4).

Students can begin to sort through the confusing lists of concepts contained within the five themes by compiling lists of essential terms under each theme. The unsorted list for *place*, for example, might look like this: *human characteristics, roads, traditions, climate, plants, buildings, languages, soil, wildlife, physical characteristics, waterways, economics, religion, political beliefs, food/agriculture*. To build understanding of the relationships among the concepts, the library media specialist or teacher can help students organize their lists visually through a "webbing" or "mapping" activity.

On the low-tech end, the librarian/teacher team simply uses a blackboard and chalk to draw a concept web. In a high-tech scenario, they demonstrate the mapping activity through the use of specialized software. Many schools use Inspiration or its elementary-level counterpart, Kidspiration, to create visually attractive concept maps.

Another option is to generate a bare-bones chart such as the one pictured in **Figure 9.2** below, in which the teaching team simply builds a Microsoft Word "Organization Chart" from the "Insert — Object" menu.

As students verbally organize the list of attributes for the theme of *place*, they quickly discover that it must first be divided into *physical characteristic*s and *human characteristics*. After filling in the first two boxes with the two main terms, students connect each additional concept to one of the two boxes.

Figure 9.2: Place Chart

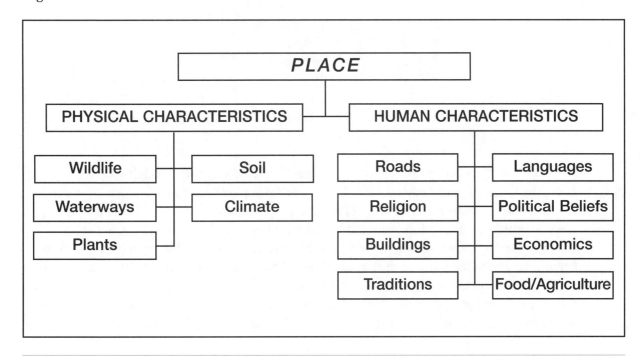

If students have access to multiple computers in the library or computer lab, they can replicate the mapping activity for each of the remaining four themes using the available organizational software. The charting activity benefits students in three ways:

1. Students identify essential components of the "Five Themes."
2. Students demonstrate an understanding of relationships among the parts of each theme.
3. Students gain and communicate knowledge visually through applied technology.

Most importantly, students construct their own understandings instead of passively "learning" teacher-delivered content.

The inquiry approach to building understanding of the five themes of geography also reinforces important information literacy skills. At the most basic level, students use a variety of resources to gain information. At a much higher level, they synthesize and organize that information, then communicate their understanding in an effective visual display. Now they are ready to connect a geographic theme to another form of visual communication—painting.

How to "Read" a Painting

Just as students must acquire specialized word attack skills to read text, so must they learn "the basic vocabularies, materials, tools, techniques, and intellectual methods" (ARTSEDGE, par. 62) of art in order to "read" a painting effectively. Artists use a common set of *elements* in their work, arranging them according to a set of artistic *principles* to attain the desired effect. In order to describe and analyze a painting, students need some familiarity with the elements and principles listed briefly below:

ELEMENTS	PRINCIPLES
Line	Balance
Shape	Harmony/unity
Form	Emphasis
Space	Movement
Texture	Proportion
Color	Rhythm
Value	Contrast
Pattern	

If the librarian or teacher feels ill-prepared to lead students through art analysis exercises, the librarian might rely on the role of "catalyst for collaboration" (*Information Power: Building Partnerships for Learning* 51) to solicit the support of the school's art teacher. Beyond building relationships with individual teachers, the library media specialist also works to establish links among the teachers themselves. When the library media specialist keeps a finger on the pulse of the entire school, those links become a natural extension of ongoing collaborative work. The willing art teacher who introduces geography students to the elements and principles of art also sends a strong message that "forging … connections is one of the things the arts do best" (ARTSEDGE, par. 2). As stated in *Information Power*,

"Effective collaboration with teachers helps to create a vibrant and engaged community of learners, strengthens the whole school program as well as the library media program, and develops support for the school library media program throughout the whole school" (51).

Rather than lecture about the elements and principles, the facilitator (library media specialist, art teacher, or geography teacher) can again lead students through an inquiry process, moving them toward the status of budding art critics. While holding up a large art poster or projecting a computer reproduction or slide of a famous painting, the facilitator asks three simple, paired questions about the work of art:

1. What do you see first? Why?
2. What do you see second? Why?
3. What do you see third? Why?

The "Why?" questions quickly lead students to define and apply the elements and principles. When asked these questions of a popular 1863 landscape by Albert Bierstadt entitled *The Rocky Mountains, Lander's Peak*, for example, students might respond with the following observations:

1. "I see the waterfall first because it is in bright sunlight and all the trees and mountains lead toward it." Students are discovering value and line.
2. "I see the mountains second because they are really big and lighter than the rest of the painting." Students are discovering value, proportion, and contrast.
3. "I see the horses and tepees third. They are in the front on a flat grassy oval surrounded by trees and a river." Students are discovering shape, line, color, and space.

The simple three-question approach above helps the uninitiated student take the first steps toward art appreciation. Harvard education professor David N. Perkins makes the case for a more thoughtful approach to looking at art. He urges "slowing looking down" (41) to allow questions to emerge from complex works of art. He suggests the following open-ended list as an aid to expanding perceptions:

◎ Ask "What's going on here?"
◎ Look for surprises—a startling color, an odd object, an unexpected relationship.
◎ Look for mood and personality.
◎ Look for symbolism and meaning. Does the artist have a message? What might it be?
◎ Look for motion.
◎ Look for capturing a time or place.
◎ Look for cultural and historical connections.
◎ Look for space and negative space.
◎ Look for specific technical dimensions (colors, shapes, balance, line, etc.).
◎ Shift your scale. Look for the big things, the small things, overall structure, detail.
◎ Look for virtuosity.[1]

---

[1] Used with permission.

However the facilitator chooses to lead the "looking at art" discussion, at this point, students have begun to build the foundation for "The Art of Geography" project. Through concept mapping, they have demonstrated a basic understanding of the five themes of geography, and they have applied the vocabulary of art. They now have hooks on which to hang their hats. Perkins states, "Let what you know inform your looking—what you know in general, about art in particular, and about the source culture and era of the work. Let your knowledge come forward to tune your vision..." (41).

Connecting American Landscape Painting to the Five Themes

Ideally, students will have access to multiple sources for their exploration of American landscape painting. In addition to quality art reference books, the collection should include links to the hundreds of museums that display their famous works on the Web. Even the tiniest regional and city museums boast excellent paintings for this unit. Students can begin their explorations at the following online museum exhibits:

- ◉ Metropolitan Museum of Art <http://www.metmuseum.org>
- ◉ National Gallery of Art <http://www.nga.gov>
- ◉ Smithsonian Museum of American Art <http://americanart.si.edu/>
- ◉ Whitney Museum of American Art <http://www.whitney.org>
- ◉ AskArt—Information on about 28,000 American artists <http://www.askart.com/>

In the interest of time, some librarians and teachers might prefer to begin with a list of art works already categorized by geographic theme rather than to leave the selections to chance. While students will gain more artistic and geographical knowledge from searching independently for works that illustrate the five themes, sometimes time and equipment do not permit such freedom. The table in **Figure 9.3**, though far from exclusive, serves to jumpstart the exploration.

Another approach begins with a simple list of American artists known for their landscape paintings. Students conduct their own searches for actual works of art by those artists. In addition to the artists and their works listed in **Figure 9.3**, students can search for landscapes by the artists below:

Thomas Hart Benton	Childe Hassam
Albertus Browere	Martin Johnson Heade
Harrison Brown	Ransome Holdredge
John Casilear	John Hudson
William Merritt Chase	William Keith
Samuel Colman	John F. Kensett
John Steuart Curry	Chauncey F. Ryder
Charles Demuth	Charles Sheeler
Asher Durand	Jerome Thompson
George Fuller	Worthington Whittredge
Sanford Robinson Gifford	Andrew Wyeth

Figure 9.3: Paintings by Geographic Theme

Paintings by Geographic Theme

Geographic Theme	Name of Artist	Name of Painting	Date
Location	Jasper Francis Cropsey	Autumn—On the Hudson River	1860
	Thomas Chambers	Felucca Off Gibralter	~1850
	Edward Hopper	Route 6, Eastham	1941
	Georgia O'Keeffe	Purple Hills Near Abiquiu	1935
Place	George Bellows	New York, 1911	1911
	Alfred Bierstadt	Merced River, Yosemite Valley	1866
	Stuart Davis	Summer Landscape	1930
	Winslow Homer	The Red School House	1873
	Grant Wood	Stone City	1930
Human/ Environment Interaction	George Bellows	Ox Team, Matinicus	1916
	George Caleb Bingham	The Jolly Flatboatmen	1846
	Edward Hicks	The Cornell Farm	1848
	Childe Hassam	Oyster Sloop, Cos Cob	1846
	George Inness	The Lackawanna Valley	1856
Movement	George Catlin	Assinneboine Chief before and after Civilization	1861
	Nathanial Currier and James Merritt Ives	A Midnight Race on the Mississippi	1860
	Thomas Eakins	The Biglin Brothers Racing	1873/4
	Winslow Homer	The Dinner Horn	1870
Region	Frederic Edwin Church	Morning in the Tropics	1877
	Thomas Cole	View of the Mountain Pass Called the Notch of the White Mountains	1839
	Sanford R. Gifford	October in the Catskills	1880
	Thomas Moran	The Much Resounding Sea	1884

The exploration phase of the unit cannot be underestimated in terms of the discussions it engenders. When students work in pairs or small groups, they continue to develop understandings of the recently-mapped geographic themes and of art criticism. At the same time, by proposing and defending their choice of paintings, they make their own art/geography connections. To hold students accountable for their searches, the library media specialist and teacher should require them to record a minimum of five titles of art works, their artists, and the names of collections or Web sites in which they are located. All of these preparatory activities come together in a final project that reinforces the primary source analysis techniques presented throughout this book.

The Art of Geography—Final Project

When connecting art to geography, students follow an objective/subjective model similar to the "Primary Source Analysis Template" introduced in Chapter 4 (**Figure 4.2**, pages 43–44). They observe for detail, interpret the painting, and determine its relationship to one geographic theme.

Working together, the library media specialist and geography teacher may choose any of the paintings or artists listed in **Figure 9.3** to model an art and geography analysis. The example that follows features Grant Wood, a Midwest regionalist painter. Students will certainly recognize his most famous painting—the national icon, *American Gothic*. While those in mainstream art circles have often criticized Wood's paintings as quaint, anti-modern, and sentimental, students find his scenes of rural town and countryside easy to understand and relate to geographic themes.

One such Grant Wood painting, *Arbor Day* (**Figure 9.4**), depicts the annual planting of a tree outside a one-room country schoolhouse in the 1890s.

As students view a projected image of the painting or as they study it together on computer monitors in a lab, the library media specialist and teacher help students locate descriptive data such as the title, date, medium, dimensions, and the collection in which it resides. Students will be interested to learn that Grant Wood completed *Arbor Day* as a school board commission and memorial to "two schoolteachers, one of whom was known to have planted a beautiful grove of trees, one each year on Arbor Day, to shelter and shade the country schoolhouse in which she had taught …" (Corn 104). This preliminary discussion sets the stage for a subsequent brainstorming session to list objective and subjective observations, as shown below.

OBJECTIVE OBSERVATIONS	SUBJECTIVE OBSERVATIONS
curving dirt road	one-room schoolhouse
rolling hills	old-fashioned, nostalgic
green grass	teacher with students of all ages
two-horse team pulling wagon	planting a tree in spring
woman in long white dress holding small tree	ceremony, drama
children (boys) and men in blue overalls	like a stage
man digging hole with shovel	beautification of the countryside
white clapboard building with bell in cupola	students arriving by foot
hand water pump	horse-pulled wagon

Figure 9.4: *Arbor Day*

Arbor Day, Grant Wood, 1932
Oil on masonite, 24" × 30"
Copyright, Cedar Rapids, Iowa, Community School District
Memorial to Catherine Motejl and Rose L. Waterstradt, McKinley School
Courtesy of ©Estate of Grant Wood/Licensed by VAGA, New York, NY

white shed with open door	importance of education
tiny building with moon crescent on door	the good life
fence posts along road	in harmony with nature
strong light, dark shadows	turning sod to soil
patterned colors in background	pioneer spirit

When arranged side by side, the two lists stand in contrast, illustrating once again the two types of observations to be made from primary sources. In the next activity, students generate a third list to prepare them to write a paragraph that relates the painting to one of the five themes of geography. Students might argue in favor of any one of the five geographic themes for this particular painting as they seek to reach consensus. They will want to refer to their concept maps of the geographic themes in defending their choices. If they were to choose "human/environment interaction" as a theme, their list might look like the one following.

Relation to Theme of Human/Environment Interaction

- changing land by building roads
- horses as a mode of transportation
- planting and growing crops
- planting trees (a celebration)
- adapting to the Midwest environment
- livelihoods dependent on water, soil, and good weather
- buildings (school, shed, outhouse, farms, and town) change the landscape
- fences (ownership)
- agriculture sustains the community

Finally, students are ready to complete "The Art of Geography" primary source analysis in **Figure 9.5**.

The library media specialist and teacher might choose to "group write" one or more of the paragraphs depending upon the abilities and grade level of the class, or they might at this point release students to begin their own search for a painting. At any rate, students will eventually use the lists they have created as a basis for three simple paragraphs on the second page of the primary source analysis worksheet.

The library media specialist and teaching partner will readily recognize that the final product of this assignment requires an assessment that honors both analytical skills and writing skills. The evaluation should include the following student actions:

- Prints and attaches to the assignment a copy of the painting to be analyzed.
- Accurately records the basic bibliographic data.
- Shows evidence of detailed observation of the work of art.
- Recognizes the use of specific elements and principles of art in the objective and/or subjective paragraphs.
- Bases the interpretation of the work of art (subjective paragraph) on research and artistic analysis.
- Argues convincingly for the relationship of the work of art to one of the five themes of geography. Includes evidence. (This item should be weighted the most heavily.)
- Organizes paragraphs logically.
- Uses correct conventions.

Certainly, these simple assessment guidelines can be developed into a more detailed rubric. The library media specialist needs to recognize and respond to the individual preferences and styles that each teacher brings to the collaborative table. Some teachers welcome pre-designed rubrics; others view them as an imposition. It pays to be sensitive to both preferences.

The Primary Source Librarian in Action

As the last of the teaching units in this book, "The Art of Geography" challenges library media specialists to integrate two distinct disciplines to teach a single concept. The strength

The Art of Geography

Geographic Theme _____

Student Name _____

Place copy of art work here

Name of Artist _____

Name of Art Work _____

Date of Art Work _____

Medium _____

Size _____

Museum or Collection _____

Connecting Art to Geography

Paragraph 1: Write an objective description of the art work—scene, people, structures, subject, significant elements of art used, etc.

_____

_____

_____

_____

_____

Paragraph 2: Write a subjective description or interpretation of the art work—emotional reaction, how artist has applied principles of art to communicate, why and for whom artist produced art work, etc.

_____

_____

_____

_____

_____

Paragraph 3: How does the art work relate to the selected theme of geography? Use Five Themes Mapping Exercise as a guide.

_____

_____

_____

_____

_____

of the lesson lies in the connections that the students themselves forge between art and geography. It proves that the librarian need not be an expert in all content areas, but rather an expert in bringing the right people, conditions, and resources together. To guarantee the success of the unit, the library media specialist should follow the suggestions below.

The Primary Source Librarian's Checklist:

- ❏ Study the table in **Figure 9.1** to reinforce the similarities between works of art and primary sources of all kinds.
- ❏ Learn to use Inspiration or other mapping software, including Microsoft Word organization charts.
- ❏ Build a collection of Web sites and print materials of "Five Themes of Geography" teaching ideas, museum Web sites, and American landscape painting.
- ❏ Collaborate with teachers to instruct in the five themes, and model the mapping process with the mapping software. Use place as an example (**Figure 9.2**).
- ❏ Contact art teachers for basic instruction in elements and principles of art.
- ❏ Facilitate the "How to Read a Painting" exercise (with help from the art teacher).
- ❏ Hand out the examples in **Figure 9.3**, "Paintings by Geographic Theme," and ask students to refer to the list as they search for specific artists and their works.
- ❏ Help students devise search strategies for their artists and the landscape paintings.
- ❏ Model an actual art/geography analysis, brainstorming objective and subjective observations and relating them to geographic themes.
- ❏ Work with students as they complete their own analysis (**Figure 9.5**).
- ❏ Publicize "The Art of Geography" projects and the collaborating teachers in newsletters and faculty meetings.

Opportunities for extending "The Art of Geography" abound. Artistically gifted students might produce their own paintings to connect to the five geographic themes. Gifted writers might compose original poems that interpret the paintings and their geographic themes. The book *Heart to Heart: New Poems Inspired by Twentieth-Century American Art* connects forty-three distinguished American poets with works by well-known American artists. Editor Jan Greenberg explains, "Whether the words are playful, challenging, tender, mocking, humorous, sad, or sensual, each work of art, seen through the eyes of a poet, helps us look at the world around us with fresh insight" (5). It is obvious that art as a primary source can both teach and inspire.

According to historian Allan H. Scholl, "… when students read a textbook about the history and geography of the United States, they 'hear' the story of their past. And while the written word is an effective medium for introducing this information to students, it should not be the only medium. Without 'seeing' their past, students miss learning how artists bring their unique perspectives to the rich fabric of history" (v.). The school librarian who works with teachers to integrate art as a primary source with other content areas helps students mold their own unique perspectives.

Chapter

10

Bringing It Home—
The Local Primary Source Librarian

Building Local Partnerships

Collaboration—an idea central to every primary source lesson in this book—becomes far more challenging when extended beyond the immediate school community. Library media specialists hardly spend their days pondering the educational goals they share with community institutions, yet they do share many, particularly with museums. The Institute of Museum and Library Services, a federal government agency, supports the connection. Director Robert S. Martin states, "Museums and libraries play a fundamentally important role in our democratic society by supporting and enhancing education.... Museums and libraries also preserve our rich and diverse culture and history, embedded in their collections of primary sources, and transmit that heritage from one generation to the next" (Martin, par. 1). At the 2002 White House Conference on School Libraries, Dr. Vartan Gregorian concluded simply, "Libraries and museums are the DNA of our culture" (7).

As part of the same educational infrastructure, museums and school libraries can work together to reinforce each others' learning goals, but someone must initiate the contact. Who better than the library media specialist, a professional with well-developed collaborative skills and the experience of bringing learners and resources together? Whether planning primary source lessons around the scrapbook collection of a small town's historical society or the vast collections of a major city art museum, the process is essentially the same. Both parties must recognize where their interests, activities, and missions intersect. Both institutions must depend upon the communication and commitment of key players to move the collaboration forward.

A Survey of Local Institutions

A quick scan of the local community leads to a surprising assortment of potential partners, beginning with museums. According to the International Council of Museums (ICOM),

"A museum is a non-profit making, permanent institution in the service of society and of its development, and open to the public, which acquires, conserves, researches, communicates and exhibits, for purposes of study, education and enjoyment, material evidence of people and their environment." Adopting the broadest possible interpretation of the ICOM definition, the library media specialist seeks to identify every institution that holds promise for student learning through primary sources.

The library media specialist can refer to the table of "Museums and Cultural Institutions" below (**Figure 10.1**) to begin the search for partners. The sample list covers only a tiny portion of museum categories among the thousands across the country. The librarian's hunt can begin within a town, a county, a twenty-mile radius of the school, or further afield.

Museum expert G. Ellis Burcaw breaks down museums into three major categories: art, historical, and science. Art museums can be further divided into the fine arts, the applied or useful arts, and folk art (primitive, peasant, ethnic, and pioneer arts and crafts). Burcaw writes that no matter what items fill historical museums, the "essential requirement…is that objects must be collected to serve the purpose of public education" (39). He divides science museums into "technology, or science and industry, museums; and natural history museums" (39).

The library media specialist can build and annotate a list of community resources with contact information for the library's files. After a ten-minute online search of the convention and visitor's bureau Web site in her medium-sized city, the author began to build a file of the following widely varied cultural institutions:

◎ Pro Rodeo Hall of Fame
◎ American Numismatic Association Money Museum
◎ Beidleman Environmental Center
◎ Rock Ledge Ranch Historic Site

Figure 10.1: Museums and Cultural Institutions

Museums and Cultural Institutions

Aquariums	Arboreta	"The Built Environment"
Children's Museums	College Library Archives	Ethnic Organizations
Fine Arts Museums	Folk Art Museums	Folklife Centers
Historical Societies	Historic Homes	Living History Museums
Local History Libraries	Local History Museums	Military Museums
Outdoor Education Centers	Planetariums	Science Centers
Sculpture Gardens	Space Centers	Sports Halls of Fame
Wax Figure Museums	Wildlife Sanctuaries	Zoos

- Cheyenne Mountain Zoo
- May Natural History Museum (a museum of insect specimens)
- Florissant Fossil Beds National Monument
- United States Olympic Complex
- Western Museum of Mining and Industry
- Colorado Springs Pioneers Museum

Action steps include distributing the list to teachers, asking teachers how they might work with any of the institutions to integrate more primary sources into their lessons, and offering to serve as a liaison. The library media specialist can also select a single institution from a list such as the one above, then expand the information given to specific teachers to include primary source examples from the collection. The "Primary Source Memo" in **Figure 10.2** on page 128 illustrates a chatty, non-threatening approach to building support for primary source collaborations with local museums.

To expand upon the idea of connecting museum educators with school personnel, the library media specialist can also offer to host a morning brainstorming session with teachers and museum representatives. On the neutral ground of the library media center, this group of professionals can consider the following questions:

- What resources do the museums have that support the curriculum?
- Do the museums already have primary source lessons packaged for use in schools?
- How can we co-develop primary source lessons to meet standards?
- What logistical problems might we encounter? How can they be overcome?
- Could any parts of the primary source lessons be carried out online?
- How can we best serve older kids? Younger kids? Teachers?
- Which specific teachers would be willing to develop and test primary source lessons using the resources of one of the museums?
- What opportunities exist for publicizing partnerships?

Whether a school's community has one cultural institution or dozens, the library media specialist who views them as an extension of the library primary source collection is now ready to put theory into practice. Effective collaborations, however, depend upon establishing a working relationship with individuals in those institutions and gaining an understanding of their particular milieu.

The World of Museum Educators

Museum educators know that as a condition of working with K–12 schools, they must support content standards. They also know about trends toward statewide standards-based testing. Like educators everywhere, they work hard to reach diverse populations, and they understand the need to differentiate instruction. Moreover, because they base their curriculum planning on primary sources, they are experts at putting into practice the concepts underlying inquiry-based learning.

Figure 10.2: Primary Source Memo

Eagleview Middle School Library Media Center

Primary Source Memo

To: Margo Allenbach, Social Studies
       Department Chair

From: Mary Johnson, The Primary Source
       Librarian

Date: 1/10/2003

Re: Pioneers Museum Primary Sources

Margo,

The Pioneers Museum here in town has a collection of primary sources that might interest your department members:

• Photographs and artifacts from the "Negro Historical Association of Colorado Springs" for use with local history curriculum. "The group's mission is to ensure that African Americans are included as an integral part of the history of the Pikes Peak Region. Its goals are to instill a sense of pride in black youths and to expose the broader community to the culture and contributions of black people."

• Francis W. Cragin collection of 32 handwritten notebooks filled with personal interviews of early settlers and their families.

• Artifacts related to state and local history, including Ute objects, Apache objects, Anasazi objects, Van Briggle pottery, quilts, dolls, firearms, baskets, and more.

Would you like for me to attend one of your Tuesday morning meetings to discuss the possibilities of working with the museum on a lesson in primary sources? Colorado history? Local history? We could even model a primary source lesson using our new gloves and magnifying glasses with one of our Pikes Peak area historical maps.

I would also be happy to give the Pioneers Museum a call to set up an appointment to discuss possible collaborations. Maybe I could even talk someone at the museum into coming to a department meeting.

Let me know what you think. We can always stir up some fun!

—Mary

Many publicly-funded museums suffer from inadequate budgets, which means that their personnel wear multiple hats and are "way stretched" (Kennis). A single employee might coordinate school field trips, develop teaching materials, handle all marketing, do fund raising, train docents, develop special programs, and design and author the museum's Web pages. The museum contact person for schools might be a director, a curator, an archivist, or a librarian. Often, they are a "department of one."

Surprisingly, museum educators share with school librarians some of the same frustrations in working with teachers who only halfheartedly embrace resource-based learning. Says Carol Kennis, Public Programs Coordinator for the Colorado Springs Pioneers Museum, "Our programs have changed radically to meet state standards requirements, so mostly third and fourth graders visit the museum because we have Colorado history materials for the standards at that level. Unfortunately, most teachers hold off visiting the museum until *after* the state tests in March, so the educational benefit is reduced." Rather than prepare their students with pre-visit curriculum materials, they view a museum field trip as a pleasure trip or a reward to students for having survived the high-stakes testing period. It's a "drag and drop" mentality.

In their defense, many teachers have little personal experience as museum visitors, and even less as scholars of primary sources. The library media specialist who facilitates communications between teachers and museum workers can do much to transform the one-dimensional museum experience of wandering aimlessly from exhibit to exhibit. "The up-to-date museum prefers to make the visit of the school group a truly educational experience, not merely a holiday from classroom routine. Organized lessons on single topics deal with important aspects of the museum. Museum teachers (either professionals or volunteers) show and explain exhibits, and the children handle real objects" (Burcaw 159).

Older students present a special challenge to museum educators, who are frustrated by the significant drop in numbers of visits after elementary school. Even in well-funded schools, field trips are frequently limited to a single "big one" per year to a major natural history museum, an urban zoo, or perhaps an educational IMAX movie. Various constraints include scheduling difficulties, negative impact on other classes, numbers larger than a museum can handle (especially entire middle school teams), and availability and cost of transportation. Sadly, older students miss the unique role museums play in the learning continuum: "Filled with objects, artifacts, specimens, and/or interactive experiences for their visitors, [museum] exhibits and the context they create can make abstract learning relevant and alive" (Patchen, par. 13).

The library media specialist can work with groups of older students and their teachers to make museum learning accessible. In addition to a group brainstorming session focusing solely on meeting the needs of older students, other imaginative solutions might include the following:

◎ Pull out small groups of gifted and talented students or special needs students for one-car or city bus field trips.
◎ Work with two or more teachers on interdisciplinary units related to museum visits (double the learning, half the impact on other classes).
◎ Meet students for after-school museum learning.
◎ Coordinate delivery of kits or small collections of artifacts to the classroom.

- Receive and protect library displays of local artifacts from museums.
- Connect individual students with museum mentors.
- Publicize how museum programs meet content standards for older students.
- Organize an adult after-hours field trip to a local museum featuring a museum educator.

Museum Schools Lead by Example

A handful of K–12 schools across the country model intensive museum collaborations. Most, but not all, of these "museum schools" are connected to science centers, and all rest on a culture of inquiry. Teachers and museum educators work together on curriculum, honoring each others' special knowledge and skills, and they often implement alternative assessments of student learning through presentations, exhibits, portfolios, and the like. In a study of two Massachusetts museum–school partnerships, Elsa Bailey concluded, "The power of these partnerships goes beyond the projects' nuts and bolts to include how people from two different educational cultures bonded to create something powerful and innovative. Combining individual strengths and perspectives has produced a cross-fertilization enriching all participants" (16).

Sonnet Takahisa, Co-Director of the New York City Museum School, describes the museum learning model: "People who work in museums are confronted by an object in their collection—a newly-discovered dinosaur bone, a painting, a historical letter—and they begin a process of observing that object very closely and a process of questioning: How does the information from this object relate to what I already know?" Like all of the primary source lessons in this book, lessons at the New York City Museum School begin with strong questions and links to previous knowledge.

"The school is successful," Takahisa believes, "when students understand that knowledge is constructed from primary sources." The challenge is to convince others to value the concept in an era of all-important standardized test scores. "How do we begin to define the skills that kids are getting from primary sources? Rubrics for construction of knowledge?" she wonders.

This inner city public school with a 40% poverty rate values equal access to primary sources and believes that "boutique schools" should not be the only ones privileged to spend time with primary sources. *All* children can benefit from components of the curriculum. Library media specialists should familiarize themselves with the "Museum School Object Observation Exercise" adopted from the Brooklyn Museum of Art. It includes the now-familiar recording of objective and subjective observations, followed by sharing, questions, guidance from museum experts, research, and final discussion (http://www.nysut.org/ newyorkteacher/2000-2001/010314museum-exercise.html).

Online Options

When schools lack physical access to museums, the obvious option is to "go online." Just as schools are beginning to acknowledge online learning as a growing force in education today, museums both large and small have begun a major push to digitize their collections and make them available to users everywhere. In some cases, museums have benefited from national and state grants, selecting their most significant primary source collections for the complex process of digitization, developing metadata, adding searchable images and descriptions to their Web sites, etc.

In conjunction with digitization efforts, museums and cultural institutions sometimes conduct librarian and teacher training institutes. Participants explore the online primary source artifacts and develop sample teaching materials that draw upon the newly-digitized collections. As a result of numerous primary source curriculum workshops, librarians and teachers everywhere enjoy an ever-increasing wealth of learning resources on the Web for use in the classroom.

It behooves the primary source librarian to stay abreast of local digitization efforts and to promote them in schools. While researching local primary source institutions, the library media specialist should also explore their Web sites with an eye toward eventual integration of online materials into the curriculum. In addition, the Institute of Museum and Library Services keeps a nationwide list of digitization projects that they support (http://www.imls.gov/closer/cls_po.asp) along with a grants database searchable by state (http://www.imls.gov/closer/cls_sta.asp). When no training institutes appear to be available locally, the primary source librarian can still propose them to area museum educators and colleagues as one more route to bringing primary sources to the classroom.

Finally, to build knowledge about the amazing online content available through museums, library media specialists can explore the "Showcase of Featured Museums" at MuseumStuff.com (http://www.museumstuff.com/showcase/index.html). This online portal to museum information, launched in 1999, "is an experiment in developing and testing new paradigms and strategies for 'getting the word out' about what museums have to offer the public." More than just a gateway to museums, it includes links to museum news, professional resources, events, and "Fun Museum Links for Kids." The lists of fascinating and off-beat museums alone will entertain for hours. They include The Museum of Hoaxes, The Quackatorium, The Pretzel Museum, The International Museum of Toilets, The Museum of Questionable Medical Devices, and many more.

Schools assuredly do not hold a monopoly on online learning. Some of the most innovative ideas in education focus on forming bold new partnerships, online and otherwise. Experts in the museum and library communities are also looking hard at their role in the new century through community online partnerships, as seen in the following questions provided by the Institute of Museum and Library Services:

- How do you define a learning community?
- What is the capacity of museums and libraries to address lifelong learning needs?
- Who are the other players in meeting these needs?
- What models for collaboration are already out there?
- What might an informal learning infrastructure look like?
- How might technology be employed to serve new collaborations?
- How can we assure inclusion in a new learning society?
- Who else should consider these questions?

Information on how to become part of the IMLS-sponsored "national dialogue to explore the role of museums and libraries in meeting the needs of the 21st century learner" is available on their Web site at <http://www.imls.gov/whatsnew/21cl/21clintro.htm>.

More Resources for Community Partnerships

Gary Hartzell suggests a variety of tactics for working with the community in his book, *Building Influence for the School Librarian.* He writes, "See if you can develop reciprocal agreements of any kind with other agencies in your community. Museums, health organizations, galleries, youth centers, police departments, parks and recreation departments all have resources that might be useful to you..." (177). Primary sources in local collections are especially useful given the requirement for local and state history in every child's education. In addition, one cannot underestimate the power of community partnerships for building general support for school libraries and learning.

Although this chapter outlines a number of actions for becoming better informed about local institutions and the local museum scene, many national organizations also support partnerships. For example, the Veterans History Project lists "veterans and military organizations, libraries and archives, museums, oral history programs, universities, and civic organizations" (par. 3) as official local partners. Initiated by the United States Congress, the project seeks to "collect and preserve audio- and video-taped oral histories, along with documentary materials such as letters, diaries, maps, photographs, and home movies, of America's war veterans and those who served in support of them" (par. 1). It encourages students to become "Official Youth Partners" under the guidance of teachers and media specialists. This is an excellent project for building good will and community support for schools.

Other federally funded primary source efforts strengthen community ties. The National Endowment for the Humanities sponsors excellent long-term and traveling exhibitions. For instance, across the nation, students can view exhibitions on posters from the American home front during World War II, the Indian boarding school experience, early twentieth century theater and film, and Jewish women pioneers in the upper Midwest. Library media specialists should check their own state humanities council Web sites regularly for local humanities programming that supports teaching with primary sources. Primary source projects include Chatauquas, teacher institutes, community heritage programs, and history days (http://www.neh.gov/whoweare/statecouncils.html).

Figure 10.3 lists "Resources for Community Partnerships" at the federal, state, and local levels. Library media specialists can refer to the list as a source of information about community partnerships, ongoing projects, professional museum organizations, and grant writing for local collaborations. Every organization listed as a resource will lead to unique and adventurous ideas for collaborations with community partners.

The Primary Source Librarian in Action

The library media specialist who studies and forms partnerships with community museums and cultural institutions beyond the school introduces students to a broader world of ideas. Writer Alan Gartenhaus has studied the impact of museum collections that "ignite the imagination." He believes, "While any object could be used to enhance creative thinking, museum

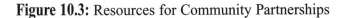

Resources for Community Partnerships

The American Association for State and Local History.
"AASLH provides leadership and support for its members who preserve and interpret state and local history in order to make the past more meaningful to all Americans." <http://www.aaslh.org/>

The Association for Living History, Farm and Agricultural Museums.
"ALHFAM is an organization of people who bring history to life. ALHFAM enables it members to make history a valuable part of the lives of museum visitors. It achieves this purpose through the exchange and sharing of ideas, information, tools and experiences centered around accurate, active, participatory, object-based historical interpretation." <http://www.alhfam.org>

Cultural Arts Resources for Teachers and Students (C.A.R.T.S.).
The newsletter of City Lore, "a cultural organization dedicated to the documentation and preservation of New York's—and America's—folk culture. The National Network for Folk Arts in Education is a network of folklorists, folk artists, and educators advocating for the full inclusion of folk and traditional arts and artists in our nation's education." <http://www.carts.org>

Institute for Museum and Library Services.
IMLS "is an independent federal agency that fosters leadership, innovation and a lifetime of learning. IMLS supports all types of museums, from art and history to science and zoos, and all types of libraries and archives, from public and academic to research and school. IMLS expands the educational benefit of these institutions by encouraging partnerships." <http://www.imls.gov>

Library of Congress American Folklife Center.
"The twentieth century has been called the age of documentation, and folklorists and other ethnographers have taken advantage of each succeeding technology, from Thomas Edison's wax-cylinder recording machine, invented in 1878, to the latest CD or digital audio equipment, in order to record the voices and music of many regional, ethnic, and cultural groups. Much of this priceless documentation has been assembled and preserved in the American Folklife Center's Archive of Folk Culture." <http://www.loc.gov/folklife/>

The National Endowment for the Humanities and the fifty-six humanities councils located in U.S. states and territories.
"NEH grants typically go to cultural institutions, such as museums, archives, libraries, colleges, universities, public television, and radio stations, and to individual scholars." Check individual states for NEH-supported exhibitions and other programs. <http://www.neh.gov>

Oral History Association.
"The Oral History Association seeks to bring together all persons interested in oral history as a way of collecting human memories….the OHA encourages standards of excellence in the collection, preservation, dissemination and uses of oral testimony. <http://www.dickinson.edu/organizations/oha/>

Veterans History Project: A Project of the American Folklife Center of the Library of Congress.
"There are 19 million war veterans living in the United States today, but every day we lose 1,500 of them. Motivated by a desire to honor our nation's war veterans for their service and to collect their stories and experiences while they are still among us, the United States Congress created the Veterans History Project." <http://www.loc.gov/folklife/vets/vets-home.html>

objects are among the highest caliber of stimuli" (9). The library media specialist can take a number of steps to bring students to the doorstep of learning through the community's primary sources.

The Primary Source Librarian's Checklist:

☐ Scan the local community for potential partners. Use **Figure 10.1** as a starting point.
☐ Develop and annotate a file of community resources with contact information.
☐ Distribute the file to teachers, asking them how they might work with the institutions to introduce more primary sources into the curriculum.
☐ Offer to serve as a liaison between organizations and key teachers. Use **Figure 10.2** as a model for collaboration.
☐ Host a brainstorming session in the library between museum personnel and teachers.
☐ Study the environments of museums and cultural institutions in order to build strong working relationships.
☐ Identify museum collections that support standards, and coordinate timely museum collaborations before statewide standards-based tests.
☐ Work together on creative solutions to counteract the drop in numbers of older students visiting museums.
☐ Study the philosophies and curricula of museum schools such as the New York City Museum School.
☐ Research current local digitization efforts, and attend librarian and teacher training institutes connected to state or local digitization projects.
☐ If no training is available, propose and coordinate local training with museum educators and school colleagues.
☐ Investigate national partnering opportunities, including those sponsored by the National Endowment for the Humanities and the American Folklife Center. Use the list in **Figure 10.3** as a starting point.
☐ Always publicize cooperative activities with local institutions.

The partnerships suggested in this chapter will help establish positive community relationships as well as creative and meaningful curriculum for students, teachers, and library media specialists. In terms of learning from the community's primary sources, students will discover that the "immediacy of the tangible object teaches, enlightens, and connects us to our heritage with a vividness and authenticity unsurpassed by any other medium" (Sheppard 8). Students of all ages will begin to think critically about primary sources as they make local connections from the past to the present to the future.

The most innovative teachers and library media specialists working today have embraced both primary sources and the models of collaboration that infuse the ideas in this book. Using the book's lessons as a springboard, educators will soon begin to create their own exciting primary source units. The library media specialist—now the school's primary source expert—capably leads the transformation.

List of Works Cited

Afflerbach, Peter and Bruce Van Sledright. "Hath! Doth! Middle Graders Reading Innovative History Text." *Journal of Adolescent & Adult Literacy*. 44.8. (May 2001): 696–707.

Alexander Graham Bell Family Papers at the Library of Congress 1862–1939. Manuscript Division, Library of Congress. 29 Sep. 2000 <http://memory.loc.gov/ammem/ bellhtml/>.

An American Ballroom Companion—Dance Instruction Manuals Ca. 1490–1920. 19 Oct. 1998 <http://memory.loc.gov/ammem/dihtml>.

American Leaders Speak: Recordings from World War I and the 1920 Election. Motion Picture, Broadcasting and Recorded Sound Division, Library of Congress. 1 Feb. 2001 <http://memory.loc.gov/ammem/nfhtml/nfhome.html>.

American Life Histories: Manuscripts from the Federal Writers' Project, 1936–1940. Manuscript Division, Library of Congress. 1996 <http://memory.loc.gov/ammem/wpaintro/>.

Antique Telephone Collectors Association. 1995 <http://atcaonline.com/>.

Bailey, Elsa. "Museum Education and Forming Partnerships with K-12 Schools." *Journal of Museum Education*. 23.2 (1998):16–18.

Barell, John. "Inquisitive Minds." *Editorial Projects in Education*. 2001. *Education Week* 14 Mar. 2001: 42, 46.

Bertel, Karen. Personal interview. 12 June 2002.

"Black History Month and Kit Themes: 2002–2010." Association for the Study of African American Life and History. <http://www.asalh.com/blackhistorytheme.htm>.

"Bloom's Taxonomy: An AskERIC Response." Syracuse University. ERIC Clearinghouse on Information & Technology. Feb. 2002 <http://www.askeric.org/cgi-bin/ printresponses.cgi/Virtual/Qa/archives/General_Education/Learning_Theories/ bloom.html>.

Blue Web'n. SBC Pacific Bell. 2003 <http://www.bluewebn.com/wired/bluewebn/>.

Boyer, Ernest L. *High School: A Report on Secondary Education in America*. The Carnegie Foundation for the Advancement of Teaching. New York: Harper & Row, 1983.

Brandt, William Nielson. *Events in Science, Mathematics and Technology*. 1994 <http://www.gsu.edu/other/timeline.html>.

Bruns, Roger A. "A More Perfect Union: The Creation of the United States Constitution." National Archives and Records Administration. 1986 <http://www.archives.gov/exhibit_hall/charters_of_freedom/constitution/ constitution_history.html>.

Burcaw, G. Ellis. *Introduction to Museum Work*. 3rd ed. Walnut Creek, CA: Altamira, 1997.

Burke, James. *Circles: Fifty Round Trips through History, Technology, Science, Culture*. New York: Simon & Schuster, 2000.

Carroll, Andrew, ed. *Letters of a Nation*. New York: Kodansha International, 1997.

"Celebrating Hispanic Heritage." The Gale Group. 2003 <http://www.galegroup.com/free_resources/chh/index.htm>.

"The Charters of Freedom." National Archives and Records Administration.
   <http://www.archives.gov/exhibit_hall/charters_of_freedom/charters_of_freedom.html>.

Christianson, Gale E. *Writing Lives is the Devil! Essays of a Biographer at Work*. Hamden,
   CN: Archon, 1993.

The Civil War Archive Union Regimental Histories Ohio. 2000
   <http://www.civilwararchive.com/Unreghst/unohinf8.htm>.

Corn, Wanda M. *Grant Wood: The Regionalist Vision*. New Haven, CT: Yale University
   Press, 1983.

"Crazy Horse." *DISCovering Multicultural America*. Gale Research, 1996. *Student Resource
   Center-Gold*. GALE Group. Eagleview Middle School Library Media Center,
   Colorado Springs, CO. 30 Mar. 2003 <http://infotrac.galegroup.com>.

Cuban, Larry. *How Teachers Taught: Constancy and Change in American Classrooms
   1890–1980*. New York: Longman, 1984.

Dempsey, Elam Franklin. Interviewed [Oct. 39?]. *American Life Histories: Manuscripts
   from the Federal Writers' Project, 1936–1940*. Manuscript Division, Library of
   Congress. 1996 <http://memory.loc.gov/ammem/wpaintro/wpahome.html>.

Digital Classroom. National Archives and Records Administration.
   <http://www.archives.gov/digital_classroom/>.

"DoHistory." Film Study Center, Harvard University. 2000 <http://www.dohistory.org>.

Douglass, Harl R. *Modern Methods in High School Teaching*. Boston: Houghton Mifflin,
   1926.

Dublin, Thomas, ed. *Farm to Factory: Women's Letters, 1830–1860*. New York: Columbia
   University, 1981.

"Epistolary Fiction." Madison Public Library. 5 Feb. 1999 <http://www.scls.lib.wi.us/
   madison/booklists/epistolary.html>.

Evans, Charles T. "Principles of Historical Document Analysis." NOVA Online. Northern
   Virginia Community College. 1998
   <http://novaonline.nv.cc.va.us/eli/evans/resources/document.html>.

Evans, Robert. *The Human Side of School Change*. San Francisco: Jossey-Bass, 1996.

The Evolution of the Conservation Movement, 1850–1920. 3 May 2002
   <http://memory.loc.gov/ammem/amrv.html>.

Expectations of Excellence: Curriculum Standards for Social Studies. National Council for
   the Social Studies. Silver Spring, MD: National Council for the Social Studies,
   1994.

Feldman, Ruth Tenzer. *Don't Whistle in School: The History of America's Public Schools*.
   Minneapolis: Lerner, 2001.

Ferenz, Kathleen. "Re: Bay Area National Digital Library Fellows Project—Lessons
   Learned." E-mail to American Memory Fellows Listserv. 21 Jun. 2001.

"The Five Themes of Geography." National Geographic Society.
   <http://www.nationalgeographic.com/resources/ngo/education/themes.html>.

"Fort Pocahontas." 1999 <http://www.fortpocahontas.org>.

Gartenhaus, Alan. *Minds in Motion: Using Museums to Expand Creative Thinking*. Davis,
   CA: Caddo Gap, 1991.

Gilbert, Peter A. "Read 'Em and Weep: Encouraging a Love of Language." *A Very Good Place to Start: Approaches to Teaching Writing and Literature in Secondary School.* Craig Thorn, ed. Portsmouth, NH: Heinemann, 1991.

Girod, Mark and Shane Cavanaugh. "Technology as an Agent of Change in Teacher Practice." *T.H.E. Journal* Apr. 2001: 40–47.

Goodwin, Doris Kearns. Foreword. *In Our Own Words: Extraordinary Speeches of the American Century.* Ed. Robert Torricelli and Andrew Carroll. New York: Kodansha International, 1999. xxi–xxiii.

Gorman, Michael E. "Alexander Graham Bell's Path to the Telephone." 1994 <http://jefferson.village.virginia.edu/albell/homepage.html>.

Greatest Engineering Achievements of the 20th Century. National Academy of Engineering. 2000 <http://www.greatachievements.org/greatachievements/indexp.html>

Greenberg, Jan, ed. *Heart to Heart: New Poems Inspired by Twentieth-Century American Art.* New York: Harry N. Abrams, 2001.

Greenwood, Janette Thomas. *The Gilded Age: A History in Documents.* New York: Oxford University, 2000.

Gregorian, Vartan. Keynote Address. Proceedings of the White House Conference on School Libraries, Washington, D. C., 4 June 2002. Washington, D.C.: Institute of Museum and Library Services, 2002. 5–11.

Guidelines for Geographic Education in the Elementary and Secondary Schools. Washington, D. C.: Association of American Geographers, 1985.

Handy, Terry and Bill Lacey. *Civil War: A Simulation of Civilian and Soldier Life during the American Civil War, 1861–1865.* Carlsbad, CA: Interaction, 1993.

Hartzell, Gary N. *Building Influence for the School Librarian.* Worthington, OH: Linworth, 1999.

"Historical Treasure Chests: A Social Studies and Language Arts Activity." Stevens Institute of Technology, Center for Improved Engineering and Science Education. 2002 <http://www.k12science.org/curriculum/treasure/index.html>.

"History in the Raw." National Archives and Records Administration, 1999. <http://www.archives.gov/digital_classroom/history_in_the_raw.html>.

Holroyd, Michael. *Works on Paper: The Craft of Biography and Autobiography.* Washington, D. C.: Counterpoint, 2002.

Hopkins, Gary. "Five Times Five: Five Activities for Teaching Geography's Five Themes." 2001. Education World, Inc. 2002 <http://www.education-world.com/a_lesson/lesson071.shtml>.

Hunter, Madeline C. *Enhancing Teaching.* New York: Macmillan College, 1994.

Information Literacy Standards for Student Learning. American Library Association and Association for Educational Communications and Technology. Chicago: American Library Association, 1998.

Information Power: Building Partnerships for Learning. American Library Association and Association for Educational Communications and Technology. Chicago: American Library Association, 1998.

International Council of Museums. "ICOM Definition of a Museum." 2002 <http://icom.museum/definition.html>.

Invent Now. National Inventors Hall of Fame. 2003 <http://www.invent.org/index.asp>.

Inventing Entertainment: The Motion Pictures and Sound Recordings of the Edison Companies. Motion Picture, Broadcasting, and Recorded Sound Division, Library of Congress. 13 Jan. 1999 <http://memory.loc.gov/ammem/edhtml/>.

Jerome and Dorothy Lemelson Center for the Study of Invention and Innovation. Smithsonian Institution. <http://www.si.edu/lemelson/>.

Johnson, Doug. "Slide Show Safety." Head for the Edge column. *The Book Report.* Mar. 1999 <http://www.doug-johnson.com/dougwri/safety.html>.

Johnson, Doug. "The Indispensable Librarian." Colorado Educational Media Association Conference. Broadmoor Hotel. Colorado Springs, CO. 18 Feb. 2000.

Johnson, Doug. *The Indispensable Librarian: Surviving (and Thriving) in School Media Centers in the Information Age.* Worthington, OH: Linworth, 1997.

Kennis, Carol, Public Programs Coordinator for the Colorado Springs Pioneers Museum. Telephone interview. 11 Dec. 2002.

KidsClick! Web Search for Kids by Librarians. Ramapo Catskill Library System. 2000 <http://sunsite.berkeley.edu/KidsClick!/>.

Kimbrough, John L. "Confederate States of America Stamps and Postal History." 2002 <http://www.jlkstamps.com/long/index2.htm#QA>.

Kuhlthau, Carol C. "Inquiry-Based Learning." Jean Donham et al. *Inquiry-Based Learning: Lessons from Library Power.* Worthington, OH: Linworth, 2001.

Kuhlthau, Carol C. "Literacy and Learning for the Information Age." *Learning and Libraries in an Information Age: Principles and Practice.* Ed. Barbara K. Stripling. Englewood, CO: Libraries Unlimited, 1999. 3–21.

Levy, David M. *Scrolling Forward: Making Sense of Documents in the Digital Age.* New York: Arcade, 2001.

Levy, Steven. "To See the World in a Grain of Sand." *Educational Leadership* Nov. 1999: 70–75.

Lightfoot, Sara Lawrence. *A World of Ideas.* Ed. Bill Moyers. New York: Doubleday, 1989.

"Lives, the Biography Resource." 2002 <http://www.amillionlives.com/>.

Lucas, Stephen E. "The Stylistic Artistry of the Declaration of Independence." National Archives and Records Administration. 1989 <http://www.archives.gov/exhibit_hall/charters_of_freedom/declaration/declaration_style.html>.

MacAskill, Ross. Weekly Bulletin. Eagleview Middle School. 3 Dec. 2001.

McKenzie, Jamie. "Biography Maker." Bellingham (Washington) Public Schools. 1997 <http://www.bham.wednet.edu/bio/biomaker.htm>.

McKenzie, Jamie. *From Now On—The Educational Technology Journal.* <http://fno.org/>.

Making of America. University of Michigan Digital Library. 2001 <http://moa.umdl.umich.edu/index.html>.

Manzo, Kathleen Kennedy. "The State of the Curriculum." *Education Week on the Web.* Editorial Projects in Education. 1999 <http://www.edweek.com/ew/vol-18/36curric.h18>.

Mapping the National Parks. 2 June 1999 <http://memory.loc.gov/ammem/gmdhtml/nphtml>.

Martin, Robert S. "Institute of Museum and Library Services Director's Message." Institute of Museum and Library Services. 2002 <http://www.imls.gov/about/abt_dirm.htm>.

"Museum School Object Observation Exercise." *New York Teacher*. 14 Mar. 2001
<http://www.nysut.org/newyorkteacher/2000-2001/010314museum-exercise.html>.

"Museums, Libraries, and the 21st Century Learner." Institute of Museum and Library
Services. 2001 <http://www.imls.gov/whatsnew/21cl/21clintro.htm>.

National Museum of the American Indian. Smithsonian Institution. 2002
<http://www.nmai.si.edu/index.asp>.

National Science Education Standards. National Academy of Sciences. 1995
<http://stills.nap.edu/html/nses/>.

National Standards for Arts Education. ARTSEDGE. The John F. Kennedy Center for the
Performing Arts, Washington, DC. <http://artsedge.kennedy-center.org/profession-
al_resources/standards/natstandards/intro.html>.

National Standards for History, Basic Edition, 1996. National Center for History in the
Schools. <http://www.sscnet.ucla.edu/nchs/standards/>.

National Women's History Project. 2002 <http://www.nwhp.org/>.

"The New York City Museum School." The Center for Arts Education. Manhattan District 2.
<http://www.cae-nyc.org/PPBook/ppb08.pdf>.

The Nineteenth Century in Print: The Making of America in Books and Periodicals. 1 Mar.
2000 <http://memory.loc.gov/ammem/ndlpcoop/moahtml>.

Oberg, Dianne. "Transforming Instructional Practice: Two Case Studies of Inquiry-based
Learning." Selected papers of the International Association of School Librarianship
Annual Conference, 2001. Seattle. 148.

O'Connor, John E., ed. *Image as Artifact: The Historical Analysis of Film and Television*.
Malabar, FL: Robert E. Krieger, 1990.

Patchen, Jeffrey. "Museums, Libraries, Schools, and Student Achievement." The White
House Colloquium on Libraries, Museums, and Lifelong Learning. 29 Oct. 2002
<http://www.imls.gov/conference/namls2002/patchen.htm>.

Perkins, David N. *The Intelligent Eye: Learning to Think by Looking at Art*. Getty Center for
Education in the Arts. Occasional Pap. 4. Los Angeles: Getty Education Institute for
the Arts, 1994.

Pipher, Mary. *The Middle of Everywhere: The World's Refugees Come to Our Town*. New
York: Harcourt, 2002.

Rendell, Kenneth W. *History Comes to Life: Collecting Historical Letters and Documents*.
Norman, OK: University of Oklahoma, 1995.

Ruenzel, David. "Past Imperfect." *Thoughtful Teachers, Thoughtful Schools: Issues and
Insights in Education Today*. Editorial Projects in Education (firm). 2nd ed. Boston:
Allyn and Bacon, 1996. 21–26.

Safire, William, ed. *Lend Me Your Ears: Great Speeches in History*. New York: W. W.
Norton, 1997.

Scholl, Allan H. *United States History and Art*. New York: Glencoe/McGraw-Hill, 1992.

Schrock, Kathleen. *Kathy Schrock's Guide for Educators*. 2003
<http://school.discovery.com/schrockguide/>.

Schrock, Kathleen. *Kathy Schrock's Guide for Educators: Teacher Helpers Assessment &
Rubric Information*. Discovery School.
<http://school.discovery.com/schrockguide/assess.html>.

Schur, Joan Brodsky. "Civil War Letters." Washington, D. C.: WETA. 2002
    <http://www.pbs.org/civilwar/classroom/lesson_letters.html>.

Sewing Machines: Historical Trade Literature in Smithsonian Collections. Smithsonian
    Institution. 2001 <http://www.sil.si.edu/DigitalCollections/Trade-Literature/
    Sewing-Machines/>.

Sheppard, Beverly. *Sustaining Our Heritage: The IMLS Achievement.* Washington, D.C.:
    Institute of Museum and Library Services, 2001.

"Showcase of Featured Museums." MuseumStuff.com.
    <http://www.museumstuff.com/showcase/index.html>.

Simpson, Carol. *Copyright for Schools: A Practical Guide.* 3rd ed. Worthington, OH:
    Linworth, 2000.

Sisk, Dorothy. "Critical Literacy Can Help in These Troubled Times." *Understanding Our
    Gifted*, Winter 2002, p. 24–25.

Small, Lawrence M. "Latino Legacies." *Smithsonian.* Aug. 2002: 14.

Smith, Diane. *Letters from Yellowstone.* New York: Viking, 1999.

Standards for the English Language Arts. National Council of Teachers of English and
    International Reading Association. 1998-2001 <http://www.ncte.org/standards/
    standards.shtml>.

Stern, Ellen Stock and Emily Gwathmey. *Once Upon a Telephone: An Illustrated Social
    History.* New York: Harcourt Brace, 1994.

Student Resource Center–Gold. Gale Group, Inc. 2003 <http://www.galegroup.com>.

Takahisa, Sonnet, Co-Director, The New York City Museum School. Telephone interview.
    10 Dec. 2002.

Tally, Bill. "History Goes Digital: Teaching With On-line Primary Sources." Center for
    Children and Technology. 1 Feb. 1997
    <http://www.techlearning.com/db_area/archives/WCE/archives/tally1.htm>.

Taxonomy of Socratic Questioning. Fermilab Education Office. 10 Sept. 1999
    <http://www-ed.fnal.gov/trc/tutorial/taxonomy.html>.

"Teaching With Documents Lesson Plan: A Date Which Will Live in Infamy — The First
    Typed Draft of Franklin D. Roosevelt's War Address." U. S. National Archives and
    Records Administration.
    <http://www.archives.gov/digital_classroom/lessons/day_of_infamy/
    day_of_infamy.html>.

Teaching with Documents: Using Primary Sources from the National Archives. Vol. 1.
    Washington, D. C.: National Archives and Records Administration and National
    Council for the Social Studies, 1989.

Teaching with Documents: Using Primary Sources from the National Archives. Vol. 2.
    Washington, D. C.: National Archives and Records Administration and National
    Council for the Social Studies, 1998.

Thornwell, Emily. *The lady's guide to perfect gentility, in manners, dress, and conversa-
    tion...also a useful instructor in letter writing.* New York: Derby & Jackson, 1857.

Tyack, David and Larry Cuban. *Tinkering toward Utopia: A Century of Public School
    Reform.* Cambridge, MA: Harvard University, 1995.

United States. Census Bureau. "Hispanic Heritage Month." <http://www.census.gov/
    Press-Release/fs97-10.html>.

United States. Department of State. International Information Programs. "African American History Month." 5 Mar. 2003 <http://usinfo.state.gov/usa/blackhis/history.htm>.

United States. Institute of Museum and Library Services. <http://www.imls.gov>.

United States. National Endowment for the Humanities. <http://www.neh.gov>.

United States. National Park Service. "Civil War Soldiers and Sailors System." <http://www.itd.nps.gov/cwss/regiments.htm>.

United States. National Park Service. "Yellowstone National Park." 2003 <http://www.nps.gov/yell/index.htm>.

United States. National Park Service. "Yellowstone Online Maps List." <http://www.nps.gov/yell/planvisit/orientation/mapslist.htm>.

United States. United States Patent and Trademark Office. "Kids' Pages." <http://www.uspto.gov/web/offices/ac/ahrpa/opa/kids/kidbright.html>.

United States. White House Office of the Press Secretary. "National American Indian Heritage Month Proclamation." George W. Bush, President. 1 Nov. 2002 <http://www.whitehouse.gov/news/releases/2002/11/20021101-7.html>.

"Using Primary Source Documents in the Classroom." Ohio Historical Society, 2003 <http://www.ohiohistory.org/resource/teachers/primary.html>.

Valenza, Joyce Kasman. *Power Tools: 100+ Essential Forms and Presentations for Your School Library Information Program*. Chicago: American Library Association, 1998.

Valley of the Shadow: Two Communities in the American Civil War. "Themes of Letters and Diaries." Virginia Center for Digital History. University of Virginia. 2001 <http://jefferson.village.virginia.edu/vshadow2/HIUS403/letters/themes.html>.

Vandervelde, Joan M. "A+ Rubric." University of Northern Iowa Online Professional Development. 2002 <http://www.uni.edu/profdev/rubrics/pptrubric.html>.

"Veterans History Project." American Folklife Center, Library of Congress. 2003 <http://www.loc.gov/folklife/vets/about.html>.

Viadero, Debra. "Thinking About Thinking." *Thoughtful Teachers, Thoughtful Schools: Issues and Insights in Education Today*. Editorial Projects in Education (firm). 2nd ed. Boston: Allyn and Bacon, 1996. 31–37.

"The War Letters." *American Experience*. Videocassette. PBS Home Video, 2001.

Weinberg, Steve. *Telling the Untold Story: How Investigative Reporters Are Changing the Craft of Biography*. Columbia, MO: University of Missouri, 1992.

White, Ronald C. Jr. "Absence of Malice." *Smithsonian*, April 2002: 109–119. Adapted from *Lincoln's Greatest Speech: The Second Inaugural*. New York: Simon & Schuster, 2002.

Whitson, Bill. Revised by M. Phillips. "Library Research Using Primary Sources." Library, University of California, Berkeley, 2002 <http://www.lib.berkeley.edu/TeachingLib/Guides/PrimarySources.html>.

Wiggins, Grant and Jay McTighe. *Understanding by Design*. Alexandria, VA: Association for Supervision and Curriculum Development, 1998.

Wiltse, C. P. Interviewed by E. E. Holm, Mariaville, NB, 3 Jan. 1939. *American Life Histories: Manuscripts from the Federal Writers' Project, 1936–1940*. Manuscript Division, Library of Congress. 19 Oct. 1998 <http://memory.loc.gov/ammem/wpaintro/wpahome.html>.

Winfrey, Carey ed. "Joyous View: A Biographer and his Subject, William Clark, Meet in St. Louis." *Smithsonian*. Aug. 2002: 9.

"Yale University Library Primary Sources Research." Primary Sources Research Colloquium in History. Yale University. 1996 <http://www.library.yale.edu/ref/err/primsrcs.htm>.

Index

About the Author

When Mary Johnson began teaching high school French in rural Iowa over thirty years ago, she never dreamed that her journey as an educator would lead her to teaching jobs in France, Germany, and Colorado and eventually to the field of school librarianship. Since receiving her MLS degree from Emporia State University in 1992, she has served as Library Media Specialist and Technology Coordinator for the 1,150 students of Eagleview Middle School in Colorado Springs. In 1995, her library program was recognized as the "Exemplary School Library Media Program" in Colorado, and more recently it has been designated a "High Performance Library" by the Colorado Power Libraries program. A frequent presenter at professional conferences, Mary also trains parents, teachers, students, and fellow librarians in information literacy, online search strategies, resource-based instructional design, technology integration, and, of course, the use of primary sources.

Mary has been married for thirty years to artist Roger Hayden Johnson. They are the parents of two grown children. Mary enjoys traveling, hiking in the Rockies, reading an eclectic mix of fiction and non-fiction, and browsing through libraries, bookstores, and art galleries.